THE
FRYER COOKBOOK
By Marian Getz

www.cookbookdesigner.com

Printed in the U.S.A.

ACKNOWLEDGEMENTS

A most sincere thank you to our wonderful HSN and TSC customers without you, there would be no cookbooks.

Thank you, Wolfgang, for your passionate leadership. To be able to work with you makes me the luckiest person I know. There is no other chef in the whole world I can think of that I would rather work for. I respect you and am incredibly proud to work for you. The fact that you possess such a witty sense of humor is just the icing on the cake.

To my husband Greg, honey, we have to have the sweetest life ever. I love you.

To Jordan and Benjamin, my boys and my daughter-in-law Lindsay, you make everything in my world so much better. You are the joy of my heart.

To Mom and Dad, my burning desire to learn the wonderful craft of cooking began when I was very little. It was and still is fueled by your generous praise as well as your appreciation. Being raised in a home dedicated to the love of God first and family second, has shaped every part of my life and I thank you for that.

Thank you to the chefs who have helped shape my career over the years, Robin Stotter, Hiroyuki "Fuji" Fujino, Steve Richard, Todd Baggett, Jeff Lavine, Angi Colbert, Alba Suarez.

When you are lucky enough to work for Wolfgang Puck, you are also ever so fortunate to work with the likes of Sydney Silverman, Mike Sanseverino, Arnie Simon, Phoebe Soong, Nicolle Brown, Jonathan Schwartz and many other wonderful people at the office.

Special thanks to our editor and photographer Daniel Koren, for your gentle patience as well as for giving my garbled words and scribbled recipes a sweet voice and story. You take such beautiful photographs. You have taken my humble food and captured it on film so that each photo makes me hungry.

Marian

In all the restaurants I have worked in, the fryer has always been an important piece of kitchen equipment. Whether you are preparing an entire meal or using the fryer to garnish a dish, it is an appliance you must have. I cannot imagine a modern kitchen without a fryer.

The textures, colors and flavors of food that come from a fryer are not possible from any other appliance. Marian's Fryer Cookbook really highlights how effective the fryer can be. Once again, Marian tapped into her knowledge as a mother and a pastry chef to provide you with a wide variety of recipes.

I know that Marian's philosophy of cooking is the same as mine – use great ingredients and make awesome food. She is always looking for something new, something fresh, something local and something seasonal. Her culinary knowledge combined with her passion for cooking is second to none. The recipes that Marian has written for the fryer cookbook will motivate you to be more creative in the kitchen.

Every kitchen needs a good collection of cookbooks that cover a wide variety of foods. Marian's fryer cookbook is a wonderful addition to your book pantry.

Wolfgang Puck

TABLE OF CONTENTS

Safety

Because deep frying involves oil that is heated to very high temperatures, caution must be used when following these recipes. Always set up and maintain a safe and organized area when frying. Most foods that are fried only require a few minutes of cooking time so it is important that you remain beside the fryer to monitor frying time.

Temperature

Frying at the correct temperature is the single most important secret to great fried food. If the temperature is too low, the food will soak up the oil and it won't become crispy. If the temperature is too high, the exterior of the food will become too brown before the center has cooked through. Always use the temperature suggested in the recipes when preparing food from this book. If you are creating your own dishes, use your fryer's manual as a guide to set the correct temperature.

Oil

Many different types of oil can be used for deep frying but it is important to use an oil that can handle high temperatures without smoking and breaking down. Extra virgin olive oil is NOT an oil that should ever be used in an electric deep fryer. Some good choices are peanut oil or canola oil. Properly maintaining the oil by straining it after each use will allow you to use the oil more than once. Strain using a mesh strainer once the oil is completely cool.

Proper Fryer Use

The most common mistake when frying foods is overcrowding the fryer basket. For best results, only fry a few pieces of food at a time. Overcrowding the basket causes a big drop in oil temperature that will make the food soggy and unattractive. It is also important to make sure that the foods you fry are as dry as possible. If frying food that is coated in batter or crust, make sure that as much excess of the coating is shaken off before frying.

Salt

The salt used in this book is Diamond Crystal Kosher Salt. It is half as salty as most other brands. This is because the grains are very fluffy and therefore not as many fit into a measuring spoon. This brand also lists "salt" as the only ingredient on the box. If you are using a different brand than Diamond Crystal Kosher Salt, simply use half the amount specified in the recipe.

Vanilla

I adore vanilla and order both my vanilla extract and vanilla beans directly from a supplier from the island of Tahiti. Tahitian beans and extracts are my favorite. I use both of these in recipes where the vanilla flavor takes center stage. If vanilla is not the star flavor, like in the Banana Beignets recipe, I use less expensive imitation vanilla which adds just the right amount of vanilla flavor and aroma without overpowering the more prominent flavors. I am also crazy about an inexpensive imitation flavoring called "Magic Line Butter Vanilla Extract" which adds an incredible sweet smell and taste to baked goods. Its aroma reminds me of how a really good bakery smells.

Chocolate

Always try to use good quality chocolate and cocoa. It is easy to find excellent chocolate at most grocery stores. It is almost impossible to find good cocoa powder locally, so I buy mine online. Please see page 156 for sources to buy my favorite chocolate.

Butter

All of the butter used in this book is unsalted. Softened butter means butter that has been left at room temperature for several hours. It should be soft enough to offer no resistance whatsoever when sliced with a knife. While there is no substitute for the pure flavor of butter, you can use a substitute such as margarine without greatly affecting the outcome of the recipes in this book.

Sugar Substitute

If you wish to use a sugar substitute, I recommend using an all natural product called Zsweet. I get it at my local health food store. While it does not bake as perfectly as regular sugar, it is the best substitute I know of. I also like agave syrup and use it in many of my recipes where a liquid form of sugar can be used.

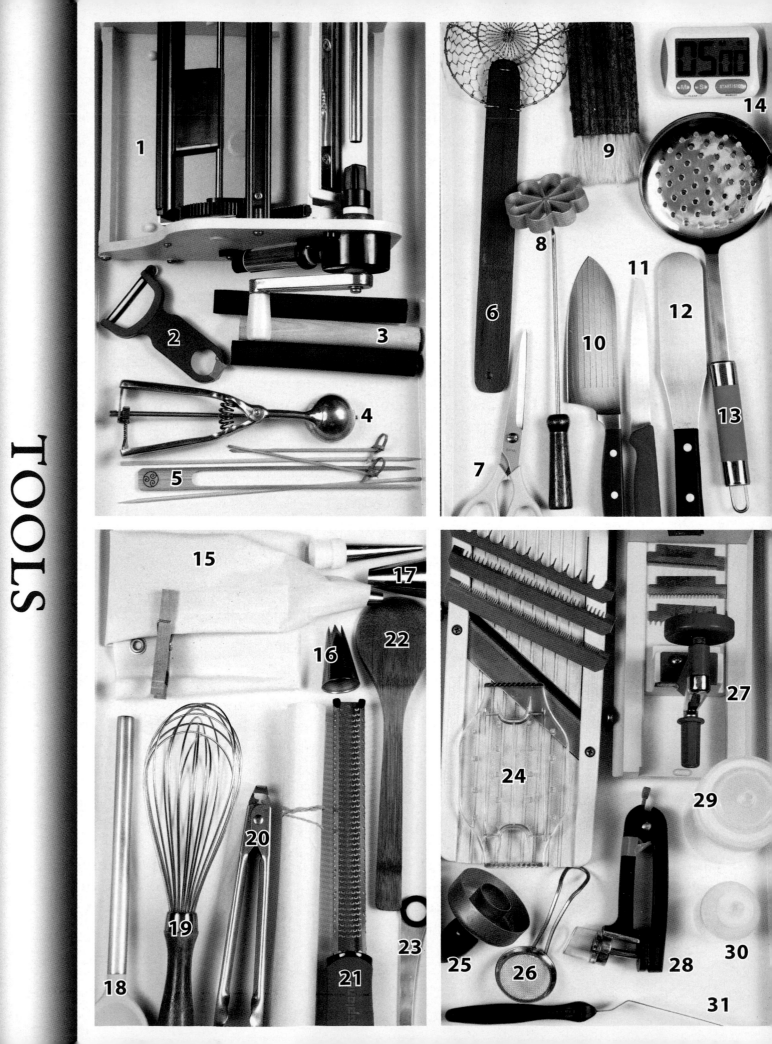

TOOLS

1. Japanese Chiba Turning Slicer (for sheets of vegetables)
2. Vegetable Peeler
3. Cannoli Dowels (before and after frying)
4. Small Ice Cream Scoop
5. Various Bamboo Skewers
6. Chinese Spider
7. Craft/Kitchen Scissors
8. Rosette Iron
9. Japanese Pastry Brush
10. 5 Inch Santoku Knife
11. Serrated Knife
12. Flat Spatula
13. American Spider
14. Digital Timer
15. Canvas Pastry Bag with Small Round Tip
16. Star Tip
17. Plain Tip
18. Silicone Coated Spoon/Spatula
19. Balloon Whisk
20. Chefs Tongs
21. Microplane Grater
22. Bamboo Spoon
23. Tornado Potato Garnish Tool
24. Japanese Mandoline
25. Donut Cutter
26. Powdered Sugar Strainer
27. Japanese Turning Slicer
28. Cherry/Olive Pitter
29. Large Squeeze Bottle
30. Small Squeeze Bottle
31. Small Offset Spatula

APPETIZERS & STREET FOODS

Fried Green Stuffed Olives

Makes 24 olives

Ingredients

Oil for frying
8 ounces cream cheese, softened
2 tablespoons fresh parsley, chopped
2 garlic cloves, minced
Zest from ½ of a lemon
24 jumbo pimento stuffed green olives, dried well

2 large eggs, beaten
1 teaspoon kosher salt
1 cup all purpose flour
1½ cups panko breadcrumbs
Lemon wheels

These full-flavored cocktail treats will be the star of your next party. They pair perfectly with martinis and will be the most talked-about food of the night. You can assemble them the day before and save the frying for the last minute so you can enjoy your guests.

1. Fill the fryer with oil and preheat to 350 degrees.

2. In a small bowl, combine the cream cheese, parsley, garlic and lemon zest; mix using a teaspoon.

3. Line a sheet pan with parchment paper.

4. Lightly flour your hands then place 2 teaspoons of the cream cheese mixture into your palm.

5. Add an olive to the center of the cream cheese and press the cheese around it until covered; place olive on the sheet pan and repeat with remaining olives.

6. Pour the eggs into a small bowl, combine the salt and flour in a separate bowl and place the panko into a third bowl.

7. Dip olives first in flour, roll them in eggs then dip them in panko until coated.

8. Place olives into the fryer basket then lower the basket into the fryer.

9. Fry for 2 minutes or until golden brown; remove and drain on absorbent paper.

10. Repeat with remaining olives and serve with lemon wheels.

Tempura Battered Vegetables

Makes 6 servings

Ingredients

Oil for frying
1 cup all purpose flour
½ teaspoon baking soda
½ cup cornstarch
1½ cups club soda
12 small asparagus spears
1 red onion, peeled and cut into thick slices

12 snow peas
6 button mushrooms, sliced
2 zucchini, sliced into rings
2 yellow squash, sliced into rings
1 carrot, peeled and sliced diagonally
1 lotus root, sliced (optional)
Kosher salt

Dipping Sauce Ingredients

¼ cup rice wine vinegar
2 tablespoons fresh lime juice
2 tablespoons granulated sugar
2 tablespoons soy sauce
1 tablespoon fresh ginger, minced
1 Thai bird chili or other red chili, julienned

4 mint leaves, julienned
4 basil leaves, julienned
1 tablespoon sesame seeds

1. Fill the fryer with oil and preheat to 350 degrees.

2. In a bowl, combine the flour, baking soda and cornstarch; stir using a whisk.

3. Add the club soda and whisk briefly (there should be lots of lumps).

4. Dip the vegetables into the batter (a few at a time); let excess drip off.

5. Place a handful of vegetables into the fryer; fry until very pale golden in color.

6. Remove and drain on absorbent paper then season with salt while still hot.

7. Repeat with remaining vegetables.

8. In a bowl, combine all dipping sauce ingredients; stir.

9. Serve vegetables with dipping sauce on the side.

Frickles

Makes 6 servings

Ingredients

Oil for frying
6 large excellent quality garlic dill pickles
1 cup yellow cornmeal
1 cup all purpose flour
1 teaspoon onion powder

1 teaspoon paprika
1 teaspoon kosher salt
1 teaspoon fresh ground black pepper
½ cup yellow mustard
¼ cup beer

Sweet & Spicy Kicked Up Ketchup Ingredients

¼ cup ketchup
2 tablespoons honey

2 teaspoons chipotle hot sauce
2 tablespoons mayonnaise

1. Fill the fryer with oil and preheat to 350 degrees.

2. Slice the pickles into thin rounds using a mandoline or food processor.

3. In a large, shallow bowl, combine the cornmeal, flour, onion powder, paprika, salt and pepper; stir.

4. In a separate bowl, combine the mustard and beer; stir.

5. Dip a handful of pickles into the mustard mixture, shake off excess mixture then drop the slices into the cornmeal mixture and shake off excess cornmeal.

6. Place the pickles into the fryer basket then lower the basket into the fryer.

7. Fry until the batter is brown and the pickles float.

8. Remove and drain on absorbent paper.

9. Repeat with remaining pickles.

10. In a bowl, combine the ketchup ingredients; stir well.

11. Serve hot with Sweet & Spicy Kicked Up Ketchup.

Punjabi Samosas

Makes 24 servings

Filling Ingredients

2 tablespoons ghee or vegetable oil

3 garlic cloves, minced

2 teaspoons fresh ginger, minced

2 large Russet potatoes, unpeeled and finely diced

1 large carrot, peeled and finely diced

2 tablespoons garam masala

1 teaspoon kosher salt

½ cup water

1 cup frozen peas

Dough Ingredients

1½ cups all purpose flour

2 teaspoons kosher salt

2 tablespoons vegetable oil

½ cup very hot water

Oil for frying

The school I attended in the Congo was called "The American School Of Kinshasa" or TASOK for short. It was a small school set on a beautiful forested campus, high in the hills above the mighty Congo River. The students were from every country around the world, which was amazing. We had several fundraisers every year. Each one had these delightfully crisp and savory Samosas for sale that the Indian as well as Pakistani moms would make. The sales at the Samosa stand were always brisk and they disappeared in no time. They smell as good as they taste.

1. In a large sauté pan over medium heat, combine the ghee, garlic, ginger, potatoes and carrots.

2. Sauté for 3 minutes then add the garam masala, salt and water; cover and cook for an additional 5 minutes or until potatoes are tender then let cool before stirring in the peas.

3. In a bowl, combine all dough ingredients, except oil for frying; mix until smooth then let rest for 5 minutes.

4. Fill the fryer with oil and preheat to 350 degrees.

5. Divide the dough into 12 balls; roll out each ball into a 6-inch circle, brush each circle with a bit of water then cut each in half.

6. Wrap the dough around your fingers to form a cone then pinch to keep it together.

7. Fill the cone with 1 tablespoon of filling; pinch to close the edges then repeat to make remaining cones.

8. Place 4 cones into the fryer; fry for 4 minutes or until brown and blistered.

9. Remove and drain on absorbent paper; repeat with remaining cones before serving.

Zellwood Sweet Corn Fritters

Makes 4 servings

Ingredients

Oil for frying

3 large egg yolks

2 tablespoons unsalted butter, melted

2 cups fresh Zellwood or yellow corn kernels, divided

1 teaspoon vanilla extract

½ cup buttermilk

¼ cup granulated sugar

3 large egg whites

1½ cups all purpose flour

1½ teaspoons kosher salt

2 teaspoons baking powder

Powdered sugar or maple syrup

Greg, fell in love with these sweet corn fritters at the Zellwood Sweet Corn Festival held each summer near his hometown of Apopka, Florida. They fry them up by the thousands and people gather in long lines, eagerly waiting to buy a little paper boat full of the crispy goodness. Greg, likes them best covered so thick in powdered sugar that you wouldn't dare breathe in while taking a bite. The outside of these golden fritters are shaggy and studded with plenty of chewy corn kernels. The interior is light and meltingly tender thanks to the beaten egg whites. Zellwood sweet corn is the best in the world which is what makes these fritters so special.

1. Fill the fryer with oil and preheat to 350 degrees.

2. In a food processor, combine the yolks, butter, 1 cup of corn, vanilla, buttermilk and sugar; purée.

3. In a clean bowl, beat the egg whites using a hand mixer until stiff peaks form.

4. Pour the pureed corn mixture and remaining corn kernels into a large bowl.

5. Fold in the flour, salt and baking powder; gently fold in the egg whites.

6. Drop the batter by the tablespoon into the fryer.

7. Fry 5 at a time for 2 minutes on each side or until golden brown; remove and let drain on a wire rack set over a absorbent paper-lined sheet pan.

8. Repeat with remaining batter; serve topped with powdered sugar or maple syrup.

Tornado Potatoes

Makes 4 servings

Ingredients

Oil for frying, preferably peanut oil
4 long and skinny fingerling potatoes
6 long bamboo skewers
Kosher salt

Chipotle Dip Ingredients

¼ cup ketchup
1 tablespoon chipotle hot sauce (or more to taste)
2 tablespoons mayonnaise
1 garlic clove, minced
1 green onion, finely sliced

1. Fill the fryer with oil and preheat to 350 degrees.

2. Insert the screw end of the garnishing tool (see tools page 8 and source page 156) into the top of a potato and hold the bottom end.

3. Place the finger of your opposite hand into the hole of the tool; begin turning it around the potato; turn to make a spiral as long as possible until you get to the end.

4. Skewer the spiral with a bamboo skewer lengthwise through the center; pull the length of the spiral down the skewer to create even spaces between the spirals then repeat with remaining potatoes.

5. Place 1 spiral into the fryer; fry for 2 minutes or until golden brown.

6. Remove and drain on absorbent paper then season with salt while still hot; repeat with remaining potatoes.

7. In a bowl, combine chipotle dip ingredients; mix well.

8. Serve hot with chipotle dip on the side.

Fried Black Eyed Peas

Makes 6 to 8 servings

Ingredients

1 pound dried black eyed peas
4 garlic cloves
3 bay leaves
2 teaspoons granulated sugar
2 teaspoons chili flakes

2 teaspoons freshly cracked pepper
Water
2 teaspoons kosher salt
Oil for frying
Hot sauce

Black eyed peas are a staple here in the South and this recipe is a real treat. The cooked peas are left to dry until no moisture is on their surface then they take a quick plunge into the hot oil which crisps their exterior. This makes for a wonderful contrast in textures.

1. In a large pot, combine the black eyed peas, garlic, bay leaves, sugar, chili flakes and pepper.

2. Add water to cover the peas by 1/2 inch, bring to a gentle simmer over medium heat then simmer for 1 hour.

3. Add the salt to the pot, stir then let peas cool.

4. Drain the peas thoroughly using a colander then spread them out on a sheet pan; let dry for 1 hour.

5. Fill the fryer with oil and preheat to 350 degrees.

6. Place 1 cup of peas into the fryer basket (they must be dry to the touch).

7. Lower the basket into the fryer; fry for 3 minutes or until crispy and brown.

8. Remove and drain on absorbent paper; season with additional salt while still hot then repeat with remaining peas.

9. Serve hot or cold with hot sauce.

Crab and Sweet Corn Cakes

Makes 6 servings

Ingredients

Oil for frying
2 slices fresh white bread, crusts removed
8 ounces fresh jumbo lump crab meat
1 cup fresh sweet corn kernels
2 green onions, minced

½ teaspoon kosher salt
4 tablespoons mayonnaise
1 large egg white
1 cup yellow cornmeal
Lemon wedges

Corn and crab go so well together because both are mild and sweet in flavor. The corn kernels provide a delightful crunch to the softness of the crab. Do not use frozen or canned corn or you will lose that crunch. Dry breadcrumbs or even panko are often responsible for crab cakes turning out heavy and dry. I prefer using soft, fresh breadcrumbs as they provide the perfect binder without soaking up all the moisture the way dried breadcrumbs do.

1. Fill the fryer with oil and preheat to 350 degrees.

2. Place the bread into a food processor; pulse until very fine crumbs are achieved.

3. Transfer the breadcrumbs to a large bowl then add remaining ingredients, except cornmeal and lemon wedges; fold the mixture gently using a spoon.

4. Line a sheet pan with plastic wrap and pour the cornmeal into a shallow bowl.

5. Form the crab mixture into 12 small patties then roll them in the cornmeal until coated on all sides.

6. Place 2 patties into the fryer basket then lower the basket into the fryer.

7. Fry for 2 minutes on each side or until golden brown.

8. Remove and let crab cakes drain on absorbent paper; repeat with remaining cakes.

9. Serve hot with lemon wedges.

Coconut Shrimp

Makes 4 servings

Ingredients

Oil for frying
1½ pounds raw shrimp, tail on, peeled and deveined
1¼ cups all purpose flour
1½ teaspoons baking powder
2 teaspoons kosher salt
1 tablespoon sugar
1 cup whole milk
1 large egg
3 tablespoons unsalted butter, melted
1 cup sweetened shredded coconut

Dipping Sauce

4 ounces cream of coconut
6 tablespoons sour cream
¼ cup crushed pineapple, drained

1. Fill the fryer with oil and preheat to 375 degrees.

2. Butterfly the shrimp by cutting them lengthwise almost all the way through.

3. In a bowl, combine the flour, baking powder and salt.

4. Add the sugar, milk, egg and butter to the flour mixture; whisk until smooth.

5. Place the shredded coconut into a separate bowl.

6. Holding the shrimp by the tail, dip them into the batter; let excess batter drip off then roll shrimp in coconut until coated.

7. Place 6 shrimp into the fryer; fry for 3 minutes or until golden brown.

8. Remove and let drain on absorbent paper then repeat with remaining shrimp.

9. In a bowl, combine the dipping sauce ingredients; stir.

10. Serve shrimp with dipping sauce on the side.

Crispy Calamari with Singapore Slaw

Makes 4 servings

Calamari Ingredients

Oil for frying
1 pound cleaned squid, tubes and tentacles
1 cup buttermilk
½ cup all purpose flour
½ cup cornstarch

¼ cup semolina flour
½ teaspoon paprika
2 teaspoons kosher salt
Lime wedges

Singapore Slaw Ingredients

1 tablespoon dry mustard powder
¼ cup honey
2 teaspoons sriracha or hot sauce
¼ cup rice wine vinegar
1 tablespoon soy sauce
1 tablespoon white miso

½ teaspoon dark sesame oil
⅔ cup peanut oil
⅓ head green cabbage, julienned
1 carrot, peeled and julienned
1 cup cilantro leaves
1 tablespoon toasted sesame seeds

1. Fill the fryer with oil and preheat to 375 degrees.

2. In a bowl, combine the calamari and buttermilk.

3. In a separate bowl combine the flour, cornstarch, semolina, paprika and salt; whisk well.

4. Add a handful of calamari to the flour mixture; shake off excess flour.

5. Place the calamari into the fryer; fry for 2 minutes or until golden brown.

6. Remove and let drain on absorbent paper then repeat with remaining calamari; season to taste with additional salt.

7. To make the slaw, place the dry mustard, honey, sriracha, vinegar, soy sauce, miso, and sesame oil into a blender; mix until smooth.

8. While blending on high, pour the peanut oil into the blender until emulsified.

9. In a bowl, combine remaining slaw ingredients; add the sauce from the blender and toss.

10. Place the slaw on a large platter and top with the calamari.

11. Garnish with lime wedges, top with additional sesame seeds and serve.

Bacon Wrapped Cipollini Onions

Makes 6 servings

Ingredients

Oil for frying
12 deli-style cipollini onions, roasted
12 strips good quality bacon
12 small bamboo skewers

Wasabi Dipping Sauce Ingredients

1 tablespoon prepared wasabi paste
¼ cup good quality mayonnaise
1 green onion, finely sliced
1 tablespoon pickled ginger, chopped
1 teaspoon soy sauce
1 drop green food coloring (optional)

Cipollini are small, flat onions that are not really onions at all. They come from the grape hyacinth family and have a lovely onion taste. Their small size make them perfect for appetizers. You can find them fresh in some markets or roasted at most deli counters. The soft onions pair perfectly when wrapped in bacon and fried. The bacon gets crispy and forms a neat little blanket around the onion. These can be assembled the day before and fried at the last minute. If your bacon is really long or stretchy, you may need to cut the strips in half.

1. Fill the fryer with oil and preheat to 325 degrees.

2. Tightly wrap each onion with a strip of bacon.

3. Secure each onion with a skewer.

4. Place 6 onions into the fryer basket then lower the basket into the oil; cover with lid.

5. Fry for 3-4 minutes or until the bacon is crispy and brown.

6. Remove and drain on absorbent paper.

7. Repeat with remaining onions.

8. In a small bowl, combine sauce ingredients; mix well.

9. Serve with wasabi dipping sauce on the side.

Ham Croquettes with Jezebel Sauce

Makes 6 servings

Ingredients

Oil for frying
3 slices white bread, crusts removed
2 cups ham, cubed
8 ounces bulk pork sausage, uncooked
1 small onion, minced
2 large eggs, beaten
⅓ cup whole milk
1 tablespoon light brown sugar, packed
1 tablespoon dry mustard

Jezebel Sauce Ingredients

½ cup pineapple preserves
½ cup apple jelly
¼ cup prepared horseradish
1 tablespoon dry mustard

I am always happy to have leftover ham tucked away in my refrigerator or freezer. A recipe such as this one is why. These little ham bites are completely addictive. They are crispy on the outside, meltingly tender on the inside, salty, meaty and so satisfying. The Jezebel sauce you dip them in is a Southern specialty and *absolutely* makes this dish.

1. Fill the fryer with oil and preheat to 350 degrees.

2. Place the bread into a food processor; pulse until fine crumbs are achieved then transfer them to a large bowl.

3. Place the ham cubes into the food processor; pulse until fine then add the ham to the bowl with the breadcrumbs.

4. Add remaining ingredients to the bowl; mix until uniform in color.

5. Using a small ice cream scoop, form the mixture into balls then place a few into the fryer; fry for 3 minutes or until cooked through and well browned.

6. Remove and drain on absorbent paper then repeat with remaining balls.

7. In a small bowl, combine all sauce ingredients; whisk well.

8. Serve warm with the Jezebel sauce on the side.

Crispy Egyptian Falafel

Makes 18 balls

Falafel Ingredients

1 bag (12 ounces) dried chickpeas
Oil for frying
1 large onion, peeled and quartered
6 garlic cloves, peeled
1 teaspoon dried chili flakes
2 teaspoons whole cumin seeds
1 tablespoon whole coriander seeds
½ cup fresh Italian parsley leaves
½ cup fresh cilantro leaves
2 tablespoons tahini
1 tablespoon fresh lemon juice
1 teaspoon baking powder
1 tablespoon kosher salt

Tahini Dipping Sauce Ingredients

½ cup tahini
½ cup Greek yogurt
2 teaspoons fresh lemon juice
1 teaspoon honey
½ teaspoon kosher salt
¼ teaspoon cayenne pepper
1 teaspoon soy sauce

1. Soak chickpeas for 12 hours in cold water then rinse but do not cook.

2. Fill the fryer with oil and preheat to 375 degrees.

3. Place the chickpeas and remaining falafel ingredients into a food processor.

4. Pulse until evenly combined and chickpeas are small; do not purée too finely.

5. Use a small ice cream scoop to form the mixture into round balls.

6. Place 6 balls into the fryer; fry for 4 minutes or until dark brown on all sides.

7. Remove and let drain on absorbent paper.

8. Repeat with remaining mixture.

9. In a bowl, combine tahini dipping sauce ingredients.

10. Serve falafel with dipping sauce on the side.

Dressed-Up Buffalo Wings

Makes 4 servings

Ingredients

12 chicken wings
⅓ cup kosher salt, for the brine
3 cups water
Oil for frying
1½ cups all purpose flour
2 teaspoons kosher salt
1 teaspoon freshly cracked black pepper

1 teaspoon onion powder
½ teaspoon dry sage
½ teaspoon paprika
½ cup unsalted butter, melted
½ cup bottled hot sauce
⅓ cup Maytag blue cheese, crumbled
1 celery stalk, thinly sliced

1. Using a knife, cut the wings into 3 sections; drumettes, flats and wing tips.

2. Using a small knife, cut around one end of the flats to expose the bone; trim and scrape the meat until it is loosened from the end of the bone.

3. Separate the thinner of the two bones and twist it off, leaving only one bone; push the meat down into a neat ball, making the wings as clean as possible.

4. For the drumettes, cut around the drum end to expose the bone then trim and scrape the meat, pressing it down into a compact ball.

5. In a large zipper bag, combine the wings, salt for the brine and water; shake the bag to distribute the salt evenly then let it rest for 20 minutes.

6. Fill the fryer with oil and preheat to 350 degrees.

7. In a shallow bowl, combine the flour, salt, pepper, onion powder, sage and paprika; toss.

8. Remove wings from the brine, pat dry then dredge them in the flour mixture; shake off excess flour.

9. Place wings in batches into the fryer and fry for 10 minutes or until the internal temperature reaches 165 degrees; remove and drain on absorbent paper then repeat with remaining wings.

10. In a bowl, combine the butter and hot sauce then pour it over the wings to coat.

11. Serve on a platter with blue cheese and celery on the side.

Crispy Chicken Napoleon

Makes 6 servings

Confit Ingredients

4 large chicken thighs
12 garlic cloves
4 sprigs fresh thyme
10 black peppercorns
2 teaspoons kosher salt
4 cups olive oil

Napoleon Ingredients

Oil for frying
1 package green vegetable wonton wrappers
½ cup mango or peach jam
2 tablespoons red wine vinegar
1 cup alfalfa sprouts
3 green onions, julienned
1 ripe mango, julienned

1. In a heavy 4-quart pot over medium heat, combine the confit ingredients.

2. Bring to a very gentle simmer with the lid on (the oil should barely bubble).

3. Cook for 1½ hours or until the chicken falls off the bone.

4. Let chicken cool then remove and discard the skin and bones; tear chicken into shreds.

5. Fill the fryer with oil and preheat to 375 degrees.

6. Place 3 wonton wrappers into the fryer; fry for 1 minute or until puffed and crispy.

7. Remove and drain on absorbent paper then repeat until you have 18 crispy wontons.

8. In a small bowl, combine the jam and vinegar; stir.

9. Arrange a small spoonful of the jam mixture in the center of a plate then top the jam mixture with sprouts.

10. Top the sprouts with a wonton wrapper, some chicken, green onions and mango.

11. Top with a second wonton wrapper and repeat.

12. Top with a third wonton wrapper then decorate the top with green onions.

13. Repeat with remaining ingredients and serve.

Candied Pecans

Makes 3 cups

Ingredients

6 cups water

3 cups pecan halves

Oil for frying, preferably canola

2 cups powdered sugar

2 teaspoons cayenne pepper

1 teaspoon kosher salt

½ teaspoon ground cinnamon

¼ teaspoon ground cardamom

1. In a 4-quart saucepan over medium heat, bring the water to a full boil.

2. Add the pecans to the saucepan; let simmer for 1 minute then remove from heat and let stand for 5 minutes.

3. Fill the fryer with oil and preheat to 350 degrees.

4. In a bowl, combine remaining ingredients; set aside.

5. Pour the pecans into a large colander to drain.

6. Transfer the pecans to a bowl then sprinkle with the sugar mixture to coat evenly.

7. Place half of the pecans into the fryer basket; avoid any liquid that may have accumulated at the bottom of the bowl.

8. Lower the basket into the fryer; fry for 3 minutes or until the color begins to darken (stir constantly using tongs).

9. Remove and place the pecans on a sheet pan; stir pecans using tongs to prevent them from sticking as they cool.

10. Repeat with remaining pecans.

11. Blot any excess oil and store in an airtight container for up to 3 weeks.

12. Discard the oil used in this recipe.

Chili Lime Almonds and Cashews

Makes 8 servings

Ingredients

Oil for frying
2 whole garlic heads
1 pound raw almonds
1 pound raw cashews
8 dried whole red chilies
4 sprigs fresh thyme
Zest and juice of 1 lime
1 tablespoon kosher salt

Addictive is the best way to describe these nuts. A snack this good, you won't need to make any other snacks to serve your friends during a gathering. They are spicy, garlicky and just salty enough to encourage a second, third as well as a fourth handful. The recipe is quite easy to put together and is very forgiving, so you can easily change it to include some of your favorite flavors. The garlic cloves get sweet during frying. They are delightful when slipped from the skin and popped into your mouth. You can use almost any dried red chilies for this recipe. My favorite is "chiles de arbol", which can be found at most Mexican markets. No matter how many batches of these I make, they disappear within a day.

1. Fill the fryer with oil and preheat to 325 degrees.

2. Separate the garlic into cloves, leaving the paper still attached.

3. Place the fryer basket onto a baking tray lined with absorbent paper.

4. Place roughly ¼ of the nuts, garlic, chilies and thyme into the fryer basket.

5. Lower the basket into the fryer.

6. Fry for 4 minutes or until the nuts slightly darken and mixture is fragrant.

7. Remove and pour onto the baking tray to drain.

8. Sprinkle with some of the zest, juice and salt.

9. Repeat with remaining ingredients.

10. Serve hot or cold.

Homemade Potato Chips

Makes 4 to 6 servings

Ingredients

Oil for frying, preferably peanut oil
8 large red skinned potatoes
6 garlic cloves, finely minced
4 sprigs fresh thyme, stripped
6 fresh sage leaves, chopped
2 sprigs fresh rosemary, stripped and chopped
Kosher salt
Freshly cracked black pepper

1. Fill the fryer with oil and preheat to 350 degrees.

2. Line a sheet tray and a colander with absorbent paper; set aside.

3. Arrange all ingredients within arm's reach before beginning to fry; you will need a spider for this recipe (see tools page 8).

4. Carefully use a mandoline on a very thin setting to quickly slice 1 or 2 potatoes.

5. Blot the potatoes using absorbent paper then place them slowly into the fryer (if potatoes are very wet, the oil will climb, if it does, add the potatoes more slowly).

6. Use the spider to keep the potato slices moving in the oil so they do not stick.

7. Fry potatoes until fairly dark brown.

8. Remove and drain potatoes on the sheet tray then transfer them to the colander.

9. Sprinkle potatoes with some garlic, thyme, sage, rosemary, salt and pepper; toss to coat evenly.

10. Allow the oil to come back to temperature before frying the next batch of potatoes.

11. Repeat with remaining ingredients and serve.

Homemade Tater Tots

Makes 4 servings

Ingredients

2 cups water
3 large baking potatoes, peeled and diced
1 tablespoon unflavored gelatin
2 tablespoons instant flour, such as Wondra

½ teaspoon kosher salt
1 teaspoon onion powder (optional)
Oil for frying, preferably peanut oil

1. Pour the water into a food processor; add half of the potatoes then process until chopped into ¼-inch pieces.

2. Drain and rinse then repeat with remaining potatoes.

3. Dry potatoes and divide them in thin layers between 3 microwave-safe plates.

4. Using a small strainer, sift an even layer of gelatin over the potatoes then microwave each plate for 1 minute to melt the gelatin; let cool for 3 minutes.

5. Transfer the potatoes to a greased mixing bowl then toss using a spatula to distribute the gelatin.

6. Sprinkle the flour, salt and onion powder over the potatoes then stir to combine (the potatoes should be sticky).

7. Lay a sheet of plastic wrap on the counter, spoon a long line of the potatoes over it then roll the plastic wrap tightly over the potatoes, compressing the mixture into an 18-inch long by 1½-inch thick log; freeze for 30 minutes.

8. Fill the fryer with oil and preheat to 350 degrees.

9. Remove the potatoes from the freezer, remove the plastic wrap then slice the log into 1-inch pieces.

10. Place the potatoes in batches into the fryer; fry until crisp and golden brown.

11. Remove and drain on absorbent paper then season with additional salt while hot.

12. Repeat with remaining potatoes and serve.

Perfect French Fries

Makes 2 servings

Ingredients

Oil for frying, preferably peanut
¼ cup strained bacon fat (optional)
1¼ pounds Yukon Gold potatoes, peeled
Kosher salt
Ketchup

Aioli Ingredients

1 large egg
1 large egg yolk
1 garlic clove
2 teaspoons dry mustard
1 tablespoon fresh lemon juice
2 teaspoons kosher salt
½ cup mild olive oil
1 cup canola oil

1. Fill the fryer with oil and bacon fat if desired; do not turn it on.

2. Cut the potatoes into long 1/4-inch thick matchstick shapes.

3. Pat potatoes dry using absorbent paper.

4. Place the potatoes into the fryer basket then lower the basket into the cold oil.

5. Turn on the fryer and set the temperature to 375 degrees.

6. Gently shake the basket several times during the preheating.

7. When the oil starts bubbling, monitor the fries until they turn golden brown and crispy.

8. Remove and drain on absorbent paper; season with salt while still hot.

9. In a pitcher, combine all aioli ingredients; place the wand of an immersion blender at the bottom of the pitcher and mix until thickened.

10. Serve fries with aioli and ketchup.

Poutine

Gravy Ingredients

2 tablespoons unsalted butter
2 tablespoons all purpose flour
1¼ cups excellent quality beef stock
¼ teaspoon kosher salt
¼ teaspoon freshly ground pepper

Ingredients

Oil for frying
3 large Russet potatoes, peeled
1 cup cheese curds (see source page 156)

Poutine is served everywhere in Canada but is considered a specialty in Quebec. It is basically amazing French fries topped with fresh cheese curds and brown gravy. It is divine! The cheese curds squeak when you bite into them before they melt. The hot gravy dripping down on a crisp French fry is just luscious.

1. In a small saucepan over medium heat, combine the butter and flour; whisk until a smooth roux forms and the mixture turns light brown.

2. Add the beef stock all at once and whisk until mixture comes to a rolling boil.

3. Season with salt and pepper; set aside but keep warm.

4. Fill the fryer with oil and preheat to 325 degrees.

5. Cut the potatoes into 1/2-inch wide French fries; pat dry using absorbent paper.

6. Place half of the potatoes into the fryer basket then lower the basket into the fryer; cover with lid.

7. Fry for 4 minutes or until pale and soft; remove and repeat with remaining potatoes.

8. Raise the temperature to 375 degrees.

9. Place the first batch back into the fryer and fry for 1 minute; remove and drain on absorbent paper, season with salt then repeat with remaining fries.

10. Serve hot French fries on a platter topped with cheese curds and gravy.

Suzy-Q's with Mom's Dipping Sauce

Makes 4 to 6 servings

Ingredients

Oil for frying, preferably peanut oil
3 large Russet potatoes
Kosher salt

Dipping Sauce Ingredients

$\frac{1}{3}$ cup mayonnaise
$\frac{1}{3}$ cup ketchup
2 tablespoons yellow mustard

When my boys Jordan and Ben were small, I fell for a late-night infomercial on TV that featured a plastic gizmo that could "effortlessly" turn a potato into a mound of Suzy-Q potatoes in seconds. When it arrived, I let the boys help me make a special lunch with it. It did make mesmerizing piles of very long potato shreds. I remember stretching a single strand across my kitchen just to see how long it really was. We fried those curly potatoes and had a grand lunch. On a whim, I stirred ketchup, mustard and mayonnaise into an impromptu sauce to dip those hot fried potatoes into. Somehow it became known as "Mom's Dipping Sauce." Now I use a restaurant-quality Japanese turning slicer to make these Suzy-Q's (see source page 156).

1. Fill the fryer with oil and preheat to 325 degrees.

2. Set up a Japanese turning slicer with a larger cross cutter blade.

3. Cut the potatoes in half or thirds to fit the opening of the slicer; turn the potatoes into continuous potato strips until it stops then blot dry using absorbent paper.

4. Place some potatoes into the fryer basket then lower the basket into the fryer; fry for 4 minutes or until pale golden then remove and place them on a rimmed baking sheet.

5. Repeat with remaining potatoes then raise the fryer temperature to 375 degrees.

6. Fry potatoes for a second time in small batches for 1 minute or until brown.

7. Remove and drain on absorbent paper then season with salt while still hot.

8. In a small bowl, combine dipping sauce ingredients; stir.

9. Serve hot with the dipping sauce on the side.

Inside-Out Sweet Potato Balls

Makes 4 servings

Ingredients

Oil for frying
4 medium sweet potatoes, baked and mashed
3 tablespoons unsalted butter, softened
¼ cup light brown sugar
Pinch of kosher salt
½ teaspoon apple cider vinegar
1 teaspoon vanilla extract

½ teaspoon ground cinnamon
¼ teaspoon baking powder
1 tablespoon all purpose flour
4 large marshmallows
1 cup corn flake type cereal, crushed
1 large egg, beaten

1. Fill the fryer with oil and preheat to 350 degrees.

2. In a bowl, combine remaining ingredients, except marshmallows, cereal and egg; stir until smooth.

3. Divide the mixture into 4 piles.

4. Place a large piece of plastic wrap on the counter.

5. Using wet hands, gather up one sweet potato pile.

6. Press a marshmallow into the center then encase it in the sweet potato mixture.

7. Repeat with remaining sweet potato mixture then place them on the plastic wrap.

8. Pour the egg into a shallow bowl.

9. Place the cereal into a separate shallow bowl.

10. Dip the balls first in egg then roll them in cereal crumbs until coated evenly.

11. Place 2 balls into the fryer basket then lower the basket into the fryer.

12. Fry for 3 minutes, turning them using tongs while frying until evenly browned.

13. Remove and drain on absorbent paper; repeat with remaining balls then serve.

Crispy Vidalia Onion Rings

Makes 6 servings

Ingredients

Oil for frying
4 Vidalia onions
¼ cup granulated sugar
8 cups ice water
½ cup instant flour, such as Wondra
1 cup all purpose flour
1 teaspoon baking powder

2 teaspoons kosher salt
½ teaspoon paprika
Pinch of cayenne pepper
1 cup beer or club soda
Kosher salt
Malt vinegar

1. Fill the fryer with oil and preheat to 350 degrees.

2. Peel the onions and slice them into 1/2-inch thick slabs.

3. Separate the onion slabs into rings; combine the sugar and ice water then soak the rings for 10 minutes.

4. Remove and pat dry.

5. Sprinkle the onions with instant flour; toss to coat.

6. In a large bowl, combine the all purpose flour, baking powder, salt, paprika, cayenne pepper and beer; whisk until a smooth batter forms.

7. Dip several onion rings into the batter; shake off excess batter.

8. Place onion rings into the fryer basket then lower the basket into the fryer.

9. Fry for 3 minutes or until golden brown; stir using tongs while frying to prevent onion rings from sticking together.

10. Remove and drain on absorbent paper then sprinkle with salt while still hot.

11. Repeat with remaining onions.

12. Serve onion rings with malt vinegar on the side.

Aunt Eva's Hush Puppies

Makes 6 servings

Ingredients

Oil for frying
1½ cups yellow cornmeal
½ cup all purpose flour
2 tablespoons granulated sugar
1½ teaspoons baking powder
¼ teaspoon cayenne pepper
2 teaspoons kosher salt
1 large yellow onion, peeled and chopped

6 green onions, chopped
2 tablespoons red bell pepper, diced
3 tablespoons unsalted butter, melted
1 large egg
½ cup buttermilk
¾ cup whole milk
Kosher salt for sprinkling

Aunt Eva is the oldest of the Getz family and the proud owner of her mother's prized cast iron skillet, which has been passed down through generations. Aunt Eva says that the cast iron skillet is so seasoned with loving use that it imparts a delicious flavor to everything it cooks. I could not agree more. She makes mouth-watering Hush Puppies in it whenever the Getz family gets together for a fish fry. This usually happens when cousin Mike and uncle Philip catch fresh mullet in the shallow waters of sunny Tampa Bay. The mullets are either fried or smoked, depending on the time of year, but the hush puppies, coleslaw, grits and ice cold beer are always the accompanying side dishes. I don't have a hand-me-down heirloom cast iron skillet so I make mine in the electric deep fryer. They taste delicious either way since I'm still using Aunt Eva's recipe.

1. Fill the fryer with oil and preheat to 375 degrees.

2. In a large bowl, combine the cornmeal, flour, sugar, baking powder, cayenne pepper and salt; toss.

3. Add both onions, bell peppers, butter, egg, buttermilk and milk to the bowl; whisk well.

4. Using a small ice cream scoop, drop 6 scoops of batter into the fryer.

5. While frying, stir frequently using a spider (see tools page 8) until a deep brown color is achieved.

6. Remove and drain on absorbent paper then season with salt while still hot.

7. Repeat with remaining batter and serve.

Fried Carrot Ruffles

Makes 4 servings

Ingredients

Oil for frying
3 large carrots, peeled and cut into 3-inch lengths
2 tablespoons instant flour, such as Wondra
Kosher salt

Curry Dip Ingredients

½ cup mayonnaise
1 tablespoon honey
¼ teaspoon kosher salt
2 teaspoons curry powder
1½ teaspoons sriracha or hot sauce
1 tablespoon fresh lime juice

1. Fill the fryer with oil and preheat to 350 degrees.

2. Set a turning slicer (see tools page 8) to its thinnest flat blade.

3. Turn carrots until they have been turned into ruffles.

4. Blot them dry using absorbent paper then evenly sprinkle them with flour.

5. Place a handful of carrots into the fryer basket then lower the basket into the fryer; cover with lid.

6. Fry for 3 minutes or until brown and crispy.

7. Remove and drain on absorbent paper then sprinkle with salt while still hot.

8. Repeat with remaining carrots.

9. In a bowl, combine all curry dip ingredients; mix well.

10. Serve with curry dip on the side.

Mom's Best Fried Okra

Makes 4 servings

Ingredients

Oil for frying
1 pound fresh okra, cut crosswise ½-inch thick
2 quarts salted ice water
2 cups yellow cornmeal
1 teaspoon kosher salt
½ teaspoon freshly cracked black pepper

Mom had the most genius way of getting us to pick okra out of the garden when we would rather be swimming in the river. She would wait until we were hungry, then start talking about how delicious and crispy the fried okra was going to be as well as how she wished that she could get supper fixed quicker but she had so much to do in the kitchen. It didn't take long until we grabbed small paring knives and ran to the garden. We would cut off only the small okra, which make for the most tender, flavorful fried okra of all. I always hated the sticky, milky sap that leaked from the cut surface. The hairy stalks where the okra grew always made me itchy but it was worth it. She says that the secret to making it taste just right is to soak the cut slices in ice water first since it takes away much of the okras' inherent sliminess.

1. Fill the fryer with oil and preheat to 350 degrees.

2. Place the okra into a large bowl of salted ice water.

3. Soak for 15 minutes then drain thoroughly.

4. In a shallow bowl, combine remaining ingredients.

5. Toss a third of the okra into the cornmeal mixture; scoop them up using a spider (see tools page 8) then place them into the fryer.

6. Fry for 7 minutes or until brown and crispy.

7. Remove and drain on absorbent paper; season with additional salt while still hot.

8. Repeat with remaining okra and serve.

Batter Fried Portobello Mushroom Fries

Makes 4 servings

Ingredients

Oil for frying
4 large Portobello mushrooms
1 cup all purpose flour
1 cup beer
1 small garlic clove, minced
1 teaspoon baking powder
2 teaspoons kosher salt
½ teaspoon paprika
¼ teaspoon cayenne pepper

Dipping Sauce Ingredients

¼ cup mayonnaise
2 tablespoons balsamic vinegar

1. Fill the fryer with oil and preheat to 350 degrees.

2. Use a teaspoon to scrape out the dark gills from the underside of the mushrooms then wipe the caps.

3. Slice each mushroom across into 1/2-inch planks.

4. In a bowl, combine the flour, beer, garlic, baking powder, salt, paprika and cayenne; whisk well.

5. Dip a few mushroom pieces into the batter then place them into the fryer; fry for 2 minutes on each side or until well browned.

6. Remove and drain on absorbent paper; repeat with remaining mushroom planks.

7. In a small bowl, combine the dipping sauce ingredients; whisk well.

8. Serve with dipping sauce on the side.

Crunch-Fried Asparagus Spears

Makes 4 servings

Ingredients

Oil for frying
24 fresh asparagus spears, trimmed
1 cup all purpose flour
1½ teaspoons kosher salt
1 teaspoon freshly cracked pepper
¼ teaspoon cayenne pepper
½ teaspoon onion powder
2 large eggs, beaten
2 cups saltine crackers, ground

Butter Sauce Ingredients

Zest and juice of 1 lemon
4 tablespoons unsalted butter, melted

Asparagus is one of the best foods to serve at a party. When they are fried like in this recipe, I like to stand them upright in tall glasses and serve them with small ramekins of butter sauce for quick dipping. These can be assembled early in the day and fried at the last minute. This recipe works best with fatter asparagus rather than the pencil-thin variety.

1. Fill the fryer with oil and preheat to 375 degrees.

2. Peel the asparagus if skins are tough.

3. In a shallow bowl, combine the flour, salt, pepper, cayenne and onion powder; whisk well.

4. Pour the eggs into a separate shallow bowl and spread the cracker crumbs in a third bowl.

5. Dip each spear first in seasoned flour, shake off excess then dip them into the egg; let excess drip off then roll them in cracker crumbs until coated.

6. Place 5 spears into the fryer; fry for 2 minutes or until golden brown.

7. Remove and drain on absorbent paper then repeat with remaining asparagus.

8. In a small bowl, combine the butter sauce ingredients; stir.

9. Top asparagus with butter sauce and serve.

Black Eyed Pea Cakes

Makes 6 servings

Ingredients

1 pound black eyed peas, dried
2 bay leaves
1 smoked ham hock
Water
4 garlic cloves, minced
1 yellow onion, minced
1 red bell pepper, diced
2 teaspoons hot sauce

2 teaspoons kosher salt
1 cup all purpose flour
½ cup buttermilk
Oil for frying
3 large eggs, beaten
1½ cups panko breadcrumbs
Pepper vinegar

1. In a large pot over medium heat, combine the black eyed peas, bay leaves and ham hock; add cold water to the pot until the peas are covered by 2 inches.

2. Bring to a simmer then cook for 1½ hours or until peas are tender.

3. Drain the liquid from the peas then lightly mash them inside the pot using a wooden spoon.

4. Add the garlic, onions, bell pepper, hot sauce, salt, flour and buttermilk to the pot; stir well then chill for a minimum of 1 hour.

5. Fill the fryer with oil and preheat to 350 degrees.

6. Cover a sheet pan with plastic wrap.

7. Using an small ice cream scoop, form the chilled pea mixture into 12 cakes, place them on the sheet pan then pat them into smooth patties using your wet fingers.

8. Pour the eggs into a shallow bowl and spread the panko in a separate bowl.

9. Dip each pea cake into the eggs, let excess egg drip off then dip each cake into the panko until covered on all sides; shake off excess and place 3 cakes into the fryer.

10. Fry for 3 minutes or until well browned; remove and drain on absorbent paper then repeat with remaining pea cakes and serve with pepper vinegar.

Party Parmesan Eggplant Squares

Makes 4 to 6 servings

Ingredients

1 large eggplant, peeled, cut into 1-inch squares
3 garlic cloves
1 tablespoon extra-virgin olive oil
1 teaspoon chili flakes
2 teaspoons kosher salt
Oil for frying
2 large eggs, beaten

1 cup all purpose flour
2 tablespoons flat leaf parsley, chopped
½ cup yellow cornmeal
⅔ cup Parmesan cheese, grated
Lemon wedges

1. Place the eggplant squares into a large bowl.

2. Place the garlic, olive oil, chili flakes and salt into a food processor; process until uniform in consistency.

3. Pour the garlic mixture over the eggplant squares; toss to coat evenly then pour them into a colander.

4. Place the colander in the sink; let eggplant marinate and drain for 30 minutes.

5. Fill the fryer with oil and preheat to 350 degrees.

6. Pour eggs into a shallow bowl; in a separate bowl, combine the flour, parsley and cornmeal.

7. Pat eggplant dry then dip a handful of eggplant squares into the flour mixture; shake off excess flour then dip them into the eggs and allow excess to drip off.

8. Dip again into the flour, shake off excess then place them into the fryer basket.

9. Lower the fryer basket into the fryer; fry for 3-5 minutes or until well browned on all sides.

10. Remove and let drain on absorbent paper then immediately transfer to a platter and top with Parmesan cheese.

11. Repeat with remaining eggplant and serve warm with lemon wedges.

Fried Green Tomatoes

Makes 4 to 6 servings

Ingredients

Oil for frying

1 cup yellow cornmeal

1 teaspoon dried sage

½ teaspoon garlic powder

1 teaspoon kosher salt

1 cup all purpose flour

2 large eggs, beaten

4 large unripe tomatoes, sliced ½-inch thick

Old Fashioned Boiled Dressing Ingredients

½ cup apple cider vinegar

2 large egg yolks

¼ cup granulated sugar

2 teaspoons dry mustard powder

1 teaspoon all purpose flour

1 teaspoon kosher salt

1 teaspoon freshly ground pepper

⅓ cup heavy cream

1. Fill the fryer with oil and preheat to 375 degrees.

2. In a bowl, combine the cornmeal, sage, garlic powder and salt.

3. Place the flour into a separate bowl and pour the eggs into a third bowl.

4. Coat the tomato slices first with flour, dip them in eggs then coat them in the cornmeal mixture.

5. Place a few tomato slices into the fryer; fry for 2 minutes on each side or until golden brown.

6. Remove and drain on absorbent paper; sprinkle with additional salt while still hot.

7. Repeat with remaining tomato slices.

8. In a microwave-safe bowl, combine all dressing ingredients; whisk well.

9. Microwave for 2 minutes, whisk, microwave for an additional 2 minutes then whisk again.

10. Continue to microwave until thickened and just beginning to boil then serve with the tomatoes.

Fried Baby Artichokes with Lemon

Makes 4 servings

Ingredients

Oil for frying
8 small baby artichokes, trimmed
1 lemon, thinly sliced into rounds
4 garlic cloves, thinly sliced
2 sprigs fresh oregano
2 sprigs fresh thyme
1 teaspoon dried chili flakes (optional)
Kosher salt

Balsamic Vinaigrette Ingredients

¼ cup fruity extra virgin olive oil
2 tablespoons good quality balsamic vinegar
¼ teaspoon kosher salt

1. Fill the fryer with oil and preheat to 350 degrees.

2. Using absorbent paper, pat the artichokes and lemon slices dry.

3. Place 3 artichokes into the fryer basket then lower the basket into the fryer; cover with lid.

4. Fry for 3 minutes or until they start to brown.

5. Carefully drop a few lemon slices into the fryer.

6. Continue to fry for 1 minute then sprinkle a bit of the garlic, oregano, thyme and chili flakes over the artichokes.

7. Continue to fry until well browned.

8. Remove and drain on absorbent paper then season with salt while still hot.

9. Repeat with remaining artichokes.

10. In a bowl, combine vinaigrette ingredients; mix well.

11. Serve hot with vinaigrette.

Soft Yolk Scotch Eggs

Makes 6 servings

Ingredients

6 large eggs
Water
Oil for frying
2 large eggs, beaten

3 tablespoons all purpose flour
1½ cups panko breadcrumbs
1 pound fresh sage-flavored sausage

This recipe is traditionally made with hard cooked eggs, but I find it much more interesting when using soft boiled eggs. The method for making them is the same as for hard boiled eggs, just less cooking. Peeling them takes a bit more care, since they are soft in the middle. Scotch eggs make for a quick one-hand breakfast on-the-go and taste great hot or cold. These can easily be assembled the day before, saving just the frying for the last minute.

1. Place the eggs into a saucepan over medium heat; pour enough water into the pan so the eggs are submerged.

2. Bring to a boil and cook at a simmer for exactly 6 minutes then remove from heat and run eggs under cold water; drain then shake the saucepan to crack the surface of each egg and cover with ice water to chill.

3. Peel eggs under running water to facilitate easy removal of the shells.

4. Fill the fryer with oil and preheat to 350 degrees.

5. Pour the beaten eggs into a shallow bowl, place the flour into a separate bowl and spread the panko in a third bowl.

6. Carefully dry each egg then roll them in flour.

7. Pat 1/6th of the sausage around each egg to enclose them; roll each egg again in flour, then in egg and then in panko until covered.

8. Place 3 eggs into the fryer basket then lower basket into the fryer; fry for 3 minutes or until deep golden brown.

9. Remove and drain on absorbent paper, repeat with remaining eggs and serve.

Gooey Mozzarella Planks

Makes 4 servings

Ingredients

Oil for frying
2 large eggs, beaten
1 cup all purpose flour
2 teaspoons kosher salt
Pinch of cayenne pepper

½ teaspoon onion powder
2 cups panko breadcrumbs
1 ball (8 ounces) whole milk mozzarella,
sliced into ½-inch planks lengthwise

Tomato Sauce Ingredients

4 ripe Roma tomatoes
1 small garlic clove
4 leaves fresh basil
1 teaspoon kosher salt

½ teaspoon red wine vinegar
1 teaspoon honey
¼ cup fruity olive oil

1. Fill the fryer with oil and preheat to 375 degrees.

2. Pour the eggs into a shallow bowl.

3. In a separate shallow bowl, combine the flour, salt, cayenne pepper and onion powder.

4. Place the panko into a third shallow bowl.

5. Dip each mozzarella plank first into the flour mixture then into the eggs then into the panko until coated.

6. If desired, repeat to make a crunchier coating.

7. Place a few planks into the fryer; fry until golden brown; avoid frying for too long or the cheese with start to ooze out.

8. Remove and drain on absorbent paper then sprinkle with additional salt while hot.

9. Combine all tomato sauce ingredients in a blender; blend until smooth.

10. Serve with fresh tomato sauce on the side.

Herbed Goat Cheese Fritters

Makes 4 servings

Ingredients

Oil for frying
8 ounces goat cheese
1 garlic clove, minced
1 tablespoon fresh chives, snipped
2 teaspoons fresh oregano, chopped
3 tablespoons sundried tomatoes, chopped
¼ teaspoon kosher salt
2 large eggs, beaten
1 cup panko breadcrumbs

I can't get enough of goat cheese. These gorgeous fritters are one of my favorite ways to show it off. Even people who swear they dislike goat cheese become converts after tasting this recipe. I think it is the crispy-on-the-outside-creamy-on-the-inside part that reels people in. These make a perfect appetizer or a first course to a fancy meal.

1. Fill the fryer with oil and preheat to 350 degrees.

2. In a large bowl, mash remaining ingredients, except eggs and panko.

3. Form the mixture into small pucks or fritters.

4. Pour the eggs into a shallow bowl.

5. Place the panko into a separate shallow bowl.

6. Roll the fritters in the eggs then roll in the panko until evenly coated; let rest for 10 minutes.

7. Place the fritters into the fryer basket then lower the basket into the fryer; cover with lid.

8. Fry for 2 minutes or until golden brown.

9. Remove and drain on absorbent paper.

10. Serve warm with a small dressed mesclun green salad.

Empanadas

Makes 20 servings

Filling Ingredients

1 pound lean ground beef
1 slice white sandwich bread
2 tablespoons beef stock
2 tablespoons olive oil
2 medium yellow onions, chopped
6 garlic cloves, minced
2 teaspoons ground cumin
2 teaspoons kosher salt

1 tablespoon sriracha or hot sauce
¼ cup green olives, sliced
¼ cup dark raisins
1 bunch cilantro, chopped
Juice from 1 lime
Oil for frying
Lime wedges

Dough Ingredients

3 cups masa harina
1 cup all purpose flour
1 tablespoon kosher salt

4 tablespoons vegetable oil
1 cup cold water

1. Place the beef, bread and stock into a food processor; pulse until no pieces of bread remain.

2. In a skillet over medium heat, combine the olive oil, onions and garlic; sauté until onions are translucent then add the cumin and beef mixture.

3. Cook until the beef is cooked through then add the salt, sriracha, olives and raisins.

4. Remove from heat then add the cilantro and lime juice; let cool.

5. Fill the fryer with oil and preheat to 375 degrees.

6. In a bowl, combine the dough ingredients and knead until a smooth dough forms then divide it into 12 balls.

7. On a floured surface, roll out each ball into a 4-inch circle then spoon a tablespoon of the meat filling into the center of a dough circle.

8. Brush the dough edges with a bit of water then fold it over into a half moon; crimp the edges then repeat with remaining dough and filling.

9. Place 2 empanadas into the fryer basket then lower the basket into the fryer.

10. Fry for 2 minutes or until brown and crispy; remove and drain on absorbent paper.

11. Repeat with remaining empanadas and serve with lime wedges.

Filipino Lumpia

Makes 12 rolls

Ingredients

Oil for frying
1 package lumpia or spring roll wrappers
1 pound ground pork
5 garlic cloves, minced
1 piece (1 inch) fresh ginger, peeled and minced
4 green onions, julienned

1 carrot, peeled and finely julienned
1 tablespoon soy sauce
1 teaspoon kosher salt
½ teaspoon freshly cracked black pepper
1 large egg

My friend Mary Beth Gomez gave me this incredible recipe. I love all spring or egg rolls, even the bad ones. However, the ones from the Philippines are my very favorite. Try to find lumpia wrappers instead of the easier to find egg roll wrappers. Lumpia wrappers are round and wonderfully thin, which makes them fry up extra crispy. There are many versions of lumpia such as all vegetable or all seafood, but this seasoned pork variety with little vegetables is really special.

1. Fill the fryer with oil and preheat to 350 degrees.

2. Open, separate and cover the lumpia wrappers with a damp towel.

3. In a bowl, combine remaining ingredients; mix well to distribute the egg through the mixture.

4. Place a wrapper on the counter and place a tablespoon of the filling along the bottom edge.

5. Pat mixture into a 3-inch long finger.

6. Fold over the edge of the wrapper, tuck in the sides and roll up.

7. Wet your fingers in water and brush a bit of water over the edge of the wrapper to seal.

8. Repeat with remaining ingredients.

9. Place 4 lumpia into the fryer; fry for 4 minutes or until dark brown and filling is cooked through.

10. Remove and drain on absorbent paper then repeat with remaining lumpia before serving.

Filipino Ukoy

Makes 6 servings

Ukoy Ingredients

Oil for frying
2 cups raw, grated sweet potato
6 green onions, julienned
1¼ cups chicken stock, room temperature
1½ cups cake flour
2 teaspoons granulated sugar
2 teaspoons kosher salt
1 teaspoon baking powder
12 large raw shrimp, peeled and deveined

Dipping Sauce Ingredients

¼ cup fresh lime juice
2 garlic cloves, minced
2 teaspoons fish sauce
2 teaspoons granulated sugar
½ jalapeño pepper, minced
¼ cup cilantro leaves, roughly chopped

From 5th through 12th grade, I went to a missionary boarding school in the capital city of Kinshasa, Congo so that I could attend an English speaking school. One of the best things about the experience was the large number of different nationalities attending this school. One of my friends in 5th grade was from the Philippines. She would sometimes bring theses irresistible Ukoy to school as part of her lunch. I fell in love with these crunchy sweet potato fritters at first bite. You will too.

1. Fill the fryer with oil and preheat to 375 degrees.

2. In a bowl, combine remaining ingredients, except shrimp; do not overmix.

3. Use a very small saucer to form 2 tablespoons of the batter into a circle.

4. Place a single shrimp in the center of the batter and gently press it in.

5. Carefully slip the batter from the saucer into the fryer.

6. Repeat 2 more times and fry for 2 minutes on each side.

7. Remove and drain on absorbent paper.

8. Repeat with remaining ingredients.

9. In a bowl, combine all dipping sauce ingredients.

10. Serve with dipping sauce on the side.

ENTREES

Getz Family Southern Fried Chicken

Makes 4 to 6 servings

Brine Ingredients

4 cups buttermilk

1 cup water

1 tablespoon granulated sugar

⅓ cup kosher salt

1 teaspoon black pepper

2 teaspoons dried sage

1 bay leaf

½ teaspoon dried thyme

½ teaspoon cayenne pepper

½ teaspoon Worcestershire sauce

Chicken Ingredients

1 whole chicken, cut into 10 pieces (breast is cut into 4 pieces)

Oil for frying, preferably peanut oil

¼ cup strained bacon grease (optional)

Seasoned Flour Ingredients

3 cups all purpose flour

2 tablespoons kosher salt

1 teaspoon black pepper

1 teaspoon paprika

¼ teaspoon cayenne pepper

1. In a bowl, combine all brine ingredients; whisk well.

2. Place the chicken and brine into a extra-large zipper bag and let it soak in the refrigerator for 4 hours.

3. Fill the fryer with oil and preheat to 325 degrees; add the bacon grease if desired.

4. Drain and discard the brine.

5. In an extra-large zipper bag, combine the seasoned flour ingredients then add the chicken pieces and shake until coated completely; let rest for 10 minutes.

6. Place chicken pieces in batches into the fryer; fry for 13 minutes or until the internal temperature reaches 165 degrees on a meat thermometer.

7. Remove and drain on absorbent paper, repeat with remaining chicken and serve.

Chicken Fried Steak

Makes 4 servings

Ingredients

Oil for frying
2 cups all purpose flour
1 tablespoon kosher salt
2 teaspoons black pepper
1 large egg, beaten
1 cup buttermilk
4 (5 ounces each) cube steaks, pounded ¼-inch thick

Cream Gravy Ingredients

1 medium onion, chopped
½ teaspoon dried thyme
2 cups whole milk
½ cup beef stock

1. Fill the fryer with oil and preheat to 375 degrees.

2. In a shallow bowl, combine the flour, salt and pepper; toss.

3. Reserve 4 tablespoons of the flour mixture for the cream gravy.

4. In a separate shallow bowl, combine the egg and buttermilk; whisk well.

5. Dip each steak first in the flour mixture then in the buttermilk mixture.

6. Place one steak into the fryer; fry for 2½ minutes on each side or until crusty and brown.

7. Remove and drain on absorbent paper and repeat with remaining steaks.

8. For the gravy, preheat a large skillet over medium-high heat.

9. Add 3 tablespoons of hot oil from the fryer to the skillet then add the onions and sauté for 5 minutes or until translucent.

10. Add the reserved flour mixture to the skillet and whisk until smooth.

11. Stir in remaining gravy ingredients and bring to a boil to thicken.

12. Taste for seasoning then serve the steaks topped with gravy.

Homemade Chicken Nuggets

Makes 6 servings

Ingredients

2 boneless, skinless chicken breasts, cut into 4 pieces

2 large egg whites

1 tablespoon canola oil

1 teaspoon honey

2½ teaspoons kosher salt

1 teaspoon white vinegar

1 tablespoon yellow onions, chopped

¼ cup strong chicken stock

⅓ cup long grain rice, cooked

Oil for frying

3 large eggs, beaten

1½ cups panko breadcrumbs

1. Place the chicken and egg whites into a food processor; purée until smooth then scrape down the sides of the food processor bowl.

2. Add the oil, honey, salt, vinegar, onions, stock and rice; purée until smooth.

3. Spoon the mixture into a pastry bag then cover a sheet pan with plastic wrap.

4. Pipe out radish-sized balls of the chicken mixture onto the sheet pan; use the back of a teaspoon dipped in water to flatten the balls into disks then chill for 30 minutes.

5. Fill the fryer with oil and preheat to 350 degrees.

6. Pour the beaten eggs into a shallow bowl and place the panko into a separate shallow bowl.

7. Dip the disks into the eggs, let excess drip off then roll the disks in panko until covered on all sides.

8. Place a few nuggets into the fryer; fry for 3 minutes or until well browned and cooked through.

9. Remove and drain on absorbent paper; repeat with remaining chicken before serving.

Crunchy Sesame Chicken Salad

Makes 4 servings

Ingredients

Oil for frying, preferably peanut oil

4 egg roll skins, sliced into thin strips

Kosher salt

3 large eggs, beaten

Freshly cracked pepper

1½ cups panko breadcrumbs

2 tablespoons all purpose flour

3 tablespoons sesame seeds

4 boneless, skinless chicken breasts or thighs, thinly sliced

6 cups fresh baby spinach leaves

1 English cucumber, thinly sliced

1 small red onion, peeled and thinly sliced

1 carrot, peeled and grated

1 red bell pepper, julienned

¼ cup soy sauce

3 tablespoons honey

1 tablespoon dry mustard

3 tablespoons rice wine vinegar

½ cup canola oil

½ cup cilantro leaves

1. Fill the fryer with oil and preheat to 350 degrees.

2. Place egg roll strips into the fryer and fry until crispy and brown.

3. Remove and drain on absorbent paper then season with salt while still hot.

4. Pour the eggs into a shallow bowl; season with salt and pepper.

5. In a separate shallow bowl, combine the panko, flour and sesame seeds.

6. Dip the chicken into the eggs, let excess drip off then roll the chicken in the panko mixture until coated.

7. Place a few chicken pieces into the fryer and fry until cooked through; remove and drain on absorbent paper then repeat with remaining chicken.

8. In a large bowl, combine the spinach, cucumber, onions, carrots and bell peppers; toss and set aside.

9. In a separate bowl, combine remaining ingredients, except cilantro; whisk well.

10. Divide the salad between 4 large plates then top with chicken and egg roll strips.

11. Drizzle dressing over salads, top with cilantro and serve.

Chicken Lettuce Wraps with Prawn Crackers

Makes 4 servings

Ingredients

1 package (4 ounces) mung bean glass noodles

Oil for frying

1 box (8 ounces) prawn crackers (see source page 156)

2 tablespoons vegetable oil

4 boneless, skinless chicken thighs, diced

5 garlic cloves, minced

1 tablespoon fresh ginger, minced

2 cups button mushrooms, diced

1 can diced water chestnuts, drained

2 teaspoons sriracha or hot sauce

2 teaspoons soy sauce

1 teaspoon kosher salt

2 teaspoons dark sesame oil

6 green onions, chopped

1 head butter lettuce

2 teaspoons sesame seeds

1. Soak the noodles in warm water for 15 minutes or until soft; drain then set aside.

2. Fill the fryer with oil and preheat to 375 degrees.

3. Place 5 pawn crackers into the fryer; fry for 15 seconds or until dramatically puffed.

4. Remove and let drain on absorbent paper; repeat with remaining prawn crackers then set aside.

5. In a large skillet or wok over medium-high heat, preheat 2 tablespoons of vegetable oil.

6. Add the chicken to the skillet and stir until cooked through.

7. Add the garlic, ginger and mushrooms to the skillet and continue to stir.

8. Add the chestnuts, sriracha, soy sauce, salt and sesame oil to the skillet; stir until hot.

9. Remove from heat then stir in the green onions.

10. To serve, spoon a small pile of mung bean noodles onto the center of each lettuce leaf.

11. Top each with a prawn cracker and some of the chicken mixture.

12. Top with sesame seeds then fold them over and eat like a taco.

Thai-Style Cod Cakes

Makes 6 servings

Ingredients

Oil for frying, preferably peanut
1 pound fresh cod fillets
1 lemongrass stalk, tender part minced
4 shallots, minced
1 tablespoon fresh ginger, minced
3 garlic cloves, minced
¼ cup cilantro leaves, chopped
1 teaspoon granulated sugar
1 teaspoon bottled fish sauce
1 teaspoon kosher salt
1 Thai bird chili, minced
Lime wedges
Sriracha or hot sauce

Nuoc Cham Sauce Ingredients

4 tablespoons fresh lime juice
¼ cup bottled fish sauce
2 tablespoons rice wine vinegar
1 teaspoon kosher salt
2 tablespoons granulated sugar
1 tablespoon fresh ginger, minced
1 tablespoon sriracha or sambal oelek
2 tablespoons carrot, finely julienned
2 tablespoons daikon, finely julienned
2 tablespoons fresh mint leaves, julienned
1 tablespoon sesame seeds

1. Fill the fryer with oil and preheat to 375 degrees.

2. Place the cod into a food processor and purée coarsely.

3. Combine the cod, lemongrass, shallots, ginger, garlic, cilantro, sugar, fish sauce, salt and chili; form the mixture into 6 patties then chill for 15 minutes.

4. Place 2 patties into the fryer basket then lower the basket into the fryer.

5. Fry for 4 minutes or until dark golden brown.

6. Remove and drain on absorbent paper then repeat with remaining patties.

7. In a bowl, combine Nuoc Cham ingredients; stir.

8. Serve hot with lime wedges, sriracha and Nuoc Cham sauce.

Fish and Chips

Makes 4 servings

Beer Batter Ingredients

1 cup all purpose flour
1 teaspoon baking powder
2 teaspoons kosher salt
½ teaspoon turmeric powder

½ teaspoon paprika
¼ teaspoon cayenne powder
1 cup beer or club soda

Fish and Chips Ingredients

Oil for frying
4 (4 ounces each) fresh fish fillets such as cod, halibut or hake
Perfect French Fries (see page 48)
Malt vinegar

England claims this dish as its own but it is popular all over the world. The batter is the secret to the entire experience. It must be crispy yet tender, salty yet satisfying. This is the best deep frying batter recipe I know. It is a slightly altered version of the late and famous James Beard's recipe. Any fresh and flaky fillets will work well here.

1. In a bowl, combine the beer batter ingredients; do not overmix (a few lumps should remain).

2. Fill the fryer with oil and preheat to 375 degrees.

3. Dip the fish into the batter until evenly coated; shake off excess batter.

4. Place fillets into the fryer basket, lower the basket into the fryer and cover.

5. Fry for 4 minutes or until golden brown.

6. Remove and drain on absorbent paper.

7. Serve hot with Perfect French Fries and malt vinegar.

Fried Grouper Sandwiches

Makes 4 servings

Ingredients

Oil for frying

1½ cups club soda

2 teaspoons canola oil

1 tablespoon yellow onion, very finely minced

½ teaspoon baking soda

1 teaspoon paprika

2 teaspoons kosher salt

1 cup all purpose flour

½ cup cake flour

4 small grouper fillets

4 soft hoagie buns

Lettuce

Tomato slices

Red onion slices

Homemade tartar sauce (see page 100)

Grouper sandwiches are a popular specialty in the Tampa Bay area. They have a crunchy batter on the outside and an impeccably flaky fish on the inside. When you add a soft bun and homemade tartar sauce, this sandwich becomes a food we tend to dream about. If grouper is not available, just use any fresh and mild fish for these sandwiches. Snapper is a natural substitute but I use a handy guide called "Seafood Watch" by the Monterey Bay Aquarium that shows which fish is the best choice at any given time to enjoy or avoid based on sustainability. I keep a copy in my purse but it is also available as a free app on smart phones.

1. Fill the fryer with oil and preheat to 350 degrees.

2. In a bowl, combine the club soda, canola oil and yellow onions; whisk using a hand whisk.

3. Add the baking soda, paprika, salt and flours to the bowl; whisk to just combine (the batter should have a few lumps).

4. Pat each fish fillet dry then dip them into the batter; let excess batter drip off.

5. Place 2 fillets into the fryer; fry for 2 minutes on each side or until they are cooked through.

6. Remove and drain on absorbent paper then repeat with remaining fillets.

7. Serve on buns topped with lettuce, tomatoes, onions and homemade tartar sauce.

Baja Fish Tacos

Makes 4 servings

Ingredients

Oil for frying
8 ounces fresh snapper fillet
1 cup all purpose flour
2 tablespoons cornstarch
1 cup beer or club soda
2 teaspoons canola oil
1 jalapeño pepper, minced
1 teaspoon kosher salt

1 teaspoon baking powder
12 corn tortillas
1 large white onion, minced
1 cilantro bunch, chopped
1 large tomato, diced
½ small head green cabbage, finely shredded
Lime wedges

1. Fill the fryer with oil and preheat to 375 degrees.

2. Cut the fish into 2-inch long strips and dry thoroughly.

3. In a bowl, combine the flour, cornstarch, beer, canola oil, jalapeño, salt and baking powder (leave the batter a little lumpy).

4. Dip a few pieces of fish into the batter; let excess batter drip off then place them into the fryer.

5. Fry for 2 minutes or until crispy golden brown; remove and drain on absorbent paper then repeat with remaining fish.

6. To soften the tortillas, dip them into the fryer for 10 seconds.

7. Place a few fish pieces in the center of a tortilla then top with onions, cilantro and tomatoes; squeeze a generous amount of lime juice over the taco then top with a handful of cabbage and fold to close.

8. Repeat with remaining tacos and serve with additional lime wedges.

Crispy Whole Catfish

Makes 4 servings

Catfish Ingredients

Oil for frying
1 tablespoon kosher salt
½ teaspoon freshly cracked black pepper
½ cup cornstarch
1 cup yellow cornmeal
1 cup buttermilk
2 large eggs, beaten
1 tablespoon sriracha or hot sauce
4 small, whole catfish, cleaned

Tartar Sauce Ingredients

½ cup mayonnaise
2 tablespoons yellow onion, minced
1 tablespoon dill pickle, minced
1 tablespoon sweet pickle, minced
1 tablespoon fresh parsley, chopped
1 tablespoon fresh lemon juice
½ teaspoon kosher salt
½ teaspoon fresh cracked pepper

A favorite in the South, this crispy catfish recipe is the best I know. The Getz family always enjoys this dish on days when some of us go fishing. The homemade tartar sauce recipe makes all the difference and offers a wonderful coolness in contrast to the hot, crunchy fish.

1. Fill the fryer with oil and preheat to 350 degrees.

2. In a shallow bowl, combine the salt, pepper, cornstarch and cornmeal; stir.

3. In a separate shallow bowl, combine the buttermilk, eggs and sriracha; whisk well.

4. Season the catfish inside and out with additional kosher salt and pepper.

5. Dip the fish first in the cornmeal mixture until coated then into the buttermilk mixture then again into the cornmeal mixture.

6. Place 1 catfish into the fryer basket then lower the basket into the fryer; fry for 7 minutes or until well browned and the meat flakes easily.

7. Remove and drain on absorbent paper; repeat with remaining catfish.

8. In a bowl, combine all sauce ingredients; stir well and serve with the catfish.

Potato and Herb Wrapped Fish

Makes 4 servings

Ingredients

Oil for frying

2 large Russet potatoes, peeled

4 fish fillets (4 ounces each) such as snapper or grouper

Kosher salt

Freshly cracked black pepper

4 sprigs fresh dill

4 sprigs fresh basil

12 fresh chives

Fresh Tomato Coulis Ingredients

4 Roma tomatoes

¼ cup sundried tomatoes in oil

2 teaspoons white miso

2 garlic cloves

2 teaspoons fresh oregano leaves

2 tablespoons extra-virgin olive oil

1. Fill the fryer with oil and preheat to 350 degrees.

2. Set up a Japanese turning slicer (see tools page 8).

3. Trim the potatoes into fairly smooth, bump-free cylinders then trim the potato ends to fit the opening of the slicer; turn a potato into a long, continuous sheet.

4. Cut the strip long enough to wrap it around a fish fillet twice; center a fish fillet on top of the potato sheet and season to taste with kosher salt and pepper.

5. Arrange the dill, basil and chives on top of the fillet then fold the potato over the fillet into a bundle.

6. Secure the two open sides with toothpicks or short bamboo skewers and repeat with remaining ingredients.

7. Place 2 fillets into the fryer basket then lower the basket into the fryer.

8. Fry for 4 minutes or until well browned; remove and drain on absorbent paper then repeat with remaining fish.

9. Place all coulis ingredients into a food processor; process for 1 minute or until very smooth.

10. Serve fish with tomato coulis.

Crispy Wrapped Shrimp

Makes 6 servings

Ingredients

Oil for frying
18 extra large fresh shrimp, peeled and deveined
1 teaspoon fresh ginger, minced
2 garlic cloves, minced
½ teaspoon kosher salt
1 package (17.1 ounces) katafi
6 fresh basil leaves, julienned
Lemon wedges

Fried shrimp are always good but when you wrap them in katafi, they become oh-so-memorable. Katafi is the same as phyllo dough, just shaped into long, thin shreds. It has a wonderful crunchy texture when fried that is irresistible.

1. Fill the fryer with oil and preheat to 375 degrees.

2. In a large bowl, combine the shrimp, ginger, garlic and salt; toss.

3. In a separate bowl, combine the katafi and basil; toss.

4. Wrap shrimp with katafi threads to cover, starting at the tail of the shrimp (it is not important that all of the threads adhere to the shrimp).

5. Repeat with remaining shrimp.

6. Place 4 shrimp into the fryer basket then lower the basket into the fryer; cover with the lid.

7. Fry for 3 minutes or until the katafi is golden brown and crispy.

8. Remove and drain on absorbent paper.

9. Repeat with remaining shrimp and serve with lemon wedges.

Fried Clams

Makes 4 servings

Ingredients

Oil for frying
½ cup all purpose flour
½ cup cornstarch
2 teaspoons kosher salt
½ teaspoon black pepper
2 cups dry saltine crackers, finely ground
2 large eggs, beaten
1 pint freshly shucked clams, julienned
Kosher salt
Lemon wedges

Aioli Ingredients

1 large egg
1 large egg yolk
2 garlic cloves
2 teaspoons dry mustard
2 teaspoons fresh lemon zest
1 tablespoon fresh lemon juice
2 teaspoons kosher salt
1½ cups mild olive oil

1. Fill the fryer with oil and preheat to 350 degrees.

2. In a bowl, combine the flour, cornstarch, salt and pepper; set aside.

3. Spread the cracker crumbs on a large plate and pour the eggs into a small bowl.

4. Coat the clams with the flour mixture then dredge them in eggs before rolling them in cracker crumbs.

5. Place a small handful of clams into the fryer basket then lower the basket into the fryer.

6. Fry for 1 minute on each side.

7. Remove and drain on absorbent paper, season with salt then repeat with remaining clams.

8. In a pitcher, combine all aioli ingredients.

9. Using an immersion blender at the bottom of the pitcher, mix until thick.

10. Serve with lemon wedges and aioli.

Frito Misto

Makes 4 to 6 servings

Ingredients

½ pound cleaned squid, tubes and tentacles
½ pound large scallops, halved
½ pound shrimp, peeled and deveined
½ pound fresh, small sardines, cleaned
1½ cups whole milk
2 large eggs, beaten
12 fresh sage leaves
12 fresh basil leaves

Oil for frying
1 cup all purpose flour
½ cup cornstarch
2 teaspoons kosher salt
1 teaspoon fresh black pepper
Lemon wedges

1. Rinse the squid under cold water and pat dry using absorbent paper.

2. Cut the squid tubes into ¼-inch rings.

3. Pat all the seafood dry using absorbent paper.

4. In a large bowl, combine milk, eggs, sage and basil; stir.

5. Add the seafood to the milk mixture, stir to coat then refrigerate for 30 minutes.

6. Fill the fryer with oil and preheat to 375 degrees.

7. Place flour, cornstarch, salt and pepper into a shallow bowl; mix using a fork.

8. Coat all the seafood with the flour mixture; shake off excess flour.

9. Place a handful of seafood into the fryer basket; lower the basket into the fryer.

10. Fry the seafood for 2-3 minutes or until golden brown.

11. Remove and drain on absorbent paper then season with additional salt while hot.

12. Repeat with remaining seafood and serve hot with lemon wedges.

Livers and Gizzards

Makes 6 servings

Ingredients

1 pound fresh chicken gizzards
6 cups good quality chicken stock
1 pound fresh chicken livers, cleaned
2 cups whole milk
Oil for frying
2 cups all purpose flour
1 sleeve soda crackers, crushed

2 teaspoons kosher salt
½ teaspoon freshly cracked black pepper
½ teaspoon cayenne pepper
1 teaspoon onion powder
Hot sauce
Bread & butter pickles

1. In a 4-quart saucepot over medium-low heat, combine the gizzards and chicken stock.

2. Cover the pot and bring to a simmer; let cook for 1½ hours or until gizzards are tender; set aside.

3. In a bowl combine the chicken livers and milk; let rest for 30 minutes.

4. Fill the fryer with oil and preheat to 350 degrees.

5. In a shallow bowl, combine the flour, crackers, salt, pepper, cayenne pepper and onion powder.

6. Drain the gizzards from the stock then dredge them in the flour mixture.

7. Drain the livers from the milk and dredge them in the flour mixture as well.

8. Place a handful into the fryer; fry until golden brown and livers are just cooked through.

9. Remove and drain on absorbent paper.

10. Repeat with remaining livers and gizzards.

11. Serve with hot sauce and bread & butter pickles.

Crunchy Tofu Citrus Tostadas

Makes 4 to 6 servings

Ingredients

Oil for frying
1 package (8 ounces) firm tofu, diced
2 teaspoons kosher salt
1 tablespoon mushroom soy sauce
12 small corn tortillas
1 ruby red grapefruit, segmented
1 orange, segmented
1 lime, segmented
2 cups Napa cabbage, julienned
6 radishes, very thinly sliced
½ cup cilantro leaves

Beet Vinaigrette Ingredients

1 small cooked beet, peeled and diced
1 garlic clove
½ jalapeño pepper, chopped
½ teaspoon anchovy paste
1 teaspoon fresh ginger, chopped
¼ cup rice wine vinegar
¼ cup dark agave syrup
2 teaspoons kosher salt
1 cup vegetable oil

1. Fill the fryer with oil and preheat to 375 degrees.

2. In a bowl, combine the tofu, salt and mushroom soy sauce; toss to coat evenly.

3. Place the tofu into the fryer basket and lower the basket into the fryer.

4. Fry for 3 minutes or until the edges begin to turn dark; remove and drain on absorbent paper then set aside.

5. Fry the tortillas (a few at a time) for 2 minutes or until golden brown and crisp.

6. Remove and drain on absorbent paper; season with additional kosher salt and repeat with remaining tortillas.

7. In a large bowl, combine the tofu, grapefruit, orange, lime, cabbage, radishes and cilantro; toss well.

8. In a pitcher, combine all vinaigrette ingredients; emulsify using an immersion blender then serve the tofu mixture on tortillas topped with vinaigrette.

Thai Mung Bean Noodle Salad

Makes 4 servings

Ingredients

Oil for frying
4 ounces dry mung bean noodles
½ of a green papaya, peeled and julienned
1 carrot, peeled and julienned
1 Thai bird chili, thinly sliced
3 green onions, sliced
1 cup bean sprouts, rinsed
¼ cup cilantro leaves
Lime wedges

Dressing Ingredients

¼ cup rice wine vinegar
2 teaspoons granulated sugar
2 teaspoons fish sauce
1 teaspoon white sesame seeds
1 teaspoon black sesame seeds
2 teaspoons sesame oil
1 garlic clove, minced
1 teaspoon fresh ginger, minced
½ cup neutral flavored oil

1. Fill the fryer with oil and preheat to 375 degrees.

2. Break the mung bean noodles into small clusters.

3. Place 1 cluster into the fryer (the noodles will dramatically puff up).

4. Briefly turn over the cluster of noodles.

5. Remove and drain on absorbent paper; repeat with remaining noodles.

6. In a large bowl, combine remaining ingredients, except lime wedges; toss with noodles to combine.

7. In a separate bowl, combine all dressing ingredients; stir well.

8. Top noodles with dressing and serve with lime wedges.

Indian Fry Bread

Makes 4 servings

Ingredients

Oil for frying
1 cup all purpose flour
½ teaspoon kosher salt
2 tablespoons powdered milk
1 teaspoon baking powder
½ cup water

Topping Ingredients

2 cups cooked pinto beans
2 cups cheddar cheese, shredded
2 medium tomatoes, diced
1 medium yellow onion, minced
1 head butter lettuce, shredded

The first time I had the pleasure of tasting this wonderful, chewy bread was at the Maple Leaf Festival in Baldwin, Kansas during my college years. A local group had set up a tent, complete with a giant black cauldron of hot oil. Ladies in American-Indian attire were slapping out these breads from scratch in front of me. They are like a thick flour tortilla but far chewier in a really good way. They were topped with cooked beans, lettuce, tomato and shredded cheese. They are eaten with a fork and are completely satisfying.

1. Fill the fryer with oil and preheat to 375 degrees.

2. In a large bowl, combine the flour, salt, powdered milk and baking powder.

3. Add the water to the flour mixture then stir using a fork until a dough ball forms.

4. Flour your hands and mix the dough until thoroughly combined.

5. Cut the dough into 8 pieces.

6. Using your floured hands, stretch and pat the dough into 4-inch rounds.

7. Place 1 piece of dough into the fryer.

8. Fry for 2 minutes on each side or until puffed and golden brown.

9. Remove and drain on absorbent paper.

10. Repeat with remaining dough and serve with topping ingredients or your favorite toppings.

DESSERTS

Strawberry Fritters

Makes 4 servings

Ingredients

Oil for frying

12 large strawberries, with leaves still on

1 package (2 ounces) Just Strawberries (see source page 156)

1 cup cake flour

¼ cup cornstarch

2½ teaspoons baking powder

¼ teaspoon kosher salt

1 tablespoon granulated sugar

1 teaspoon vanilla extract

1 cup cold club soda

12 bamboo skewers

I love how these fritters taste almost as much as how they look. The brilliant color (not to mention taste) comes from a product called "Just Strawberries", which are freeze dried strawberries. They add a tremendous flavor to this dish. The fritter batter gets extra tenderness from the low-protein cake flour and lightness from the club soda. Fry them up at the last minute and dust them generously with strawberry powder.

1. Fill the fryer with oil and preheat to 375 degrees.

2. Pat strawberries dry; set aside.

3. Place "Just Strawberries" into the dry bowl of a food processor; process to a fine powder (reserve 1 tablespoon of the strawberry powder for the batter and the rest for sprinkling).

4. In a bowl, combine 1 tablespoon strawberry powder, cake flour, cornstarch, baking powder, salt, sugar, vanilla and club soda; stir until a lumpy batter forms.

5. Skewer each strawberry through the green top then dip the berry almost to the top in batter; let excess batter drip off then lower the berry into the fryer.

6. Fry for 1 minute or until pale golden brown; remove and drain on absorbent paper then discard the skewer.

7. Repeat with remaining strawberries.

8. Serve hot with a generous dusting of the reserved strawberry powder.

Deep Fried Peaches

Makes 4 servings

Ingredients

Oil for frying
2 large eggs
1½ cups all purpose flour
¼ teaspoon baking powder
¼ teaspoon kosher salt
2 tablespoons brown butter, melted
2 tablespoons peach brandy

1 teaspoon fresh lemon juice
½ teaspoon vanilla extract
¾ cup club soda, ice cold
4 very ripe peaches, halved and pitted
1 cup Vanilla Sugar
Peach ice cream (optional)

Inspired by an incredible recipe for fried peaches by Jean Halberstam in an issue of the New Yorker in 2005, I have made this recipe many times. When I am at the market and smell the sweet fragrance of ripe peaches, this recipe pops into my head. The peaches fry for a short time so that they are just warmed through by the time they emerge from the frying oil covered in the crispy coating of batter. Rolling them in sugar creates a crunchy exterior that makes this sweet dessert so memorable. I love serving this with scoops of pale peach ice cream.

1. Fill the fryer with oil and preheat to 360 degrees.

2. Place the eggs into a large bowl and beat on high using a hand mixer for 2 minutes or until very light in color.

3. Reduce to the lowest speed then add the flour, baking powder, salt, butter, brandy, lemon juice and vanilla.

4. Using a hand whisk, gently fold in the club soda.

5. Dip the peaches (one at a time) into the batter and turn to coat evenly; shake off excess batter.

6. Place 1 peach into the fryer; fry for 2 minutes on each side or until golden brown.

7. Remove and drain on absorbent paper.

8. Roll in Vanilla Sugar while still hot.

9. Repeat with remaining peaches and serve with peach ice cream.

Hungarian Cherries

Makes 6 servings

Ingredients

Oil for frying, preferably peanut oil
1 pound fresh red cherries, stems on
⅓ cup half & half
⅓ cup cherry juice
3 large eggs

Pinch of ground cinnamon
¼ cup granulated sugar
1 cup cake flour
Powdered sugar

I clipped this recipe from the newspaper one summer in between my freshman and sophomore year of college. My sister Adele and I rented a tiny apartment for the summer in the small town of Greenville, Michigan. It is where I was born and it is also close to Belding, Michigan, my dad's hometown. That area is famous for growing the most delicious tart red cherries so I think it must have been cherry picking time when this recipe appeared in the paper. I am not sure why they are called "Hungarian Cherries" but these charming fried treats are addictively good. I don't know how the custom of tying the cherries in little bundles with red thread started but I love it. I have tried skipping this step but they are not nearly as charming.

1. Fill the fryer with oil and preheat to 375 degrees.

2. Wash and dry the cherries, leaving the stems intact.

3. Use red thread or ribbon to tie the stems of the cherries together in groups of three; set aside.

4. In a bowl, combine remaining ingredients, except powdered sugar.

5. Whisk until a fairly thick, smooth batter forms and only a few lumps remain.

6. Dip a cluster into the batter until the fruit is covered.

7. Place the cluster into the fryer then repeat with 3 more clusters.

8. Fry for 2 minutes or until golden brown.

9. Remove and drain on absorbent paper.

10. Repeat with remaining cherries.

11. Dust with powdered sugar and serve.

Banana Beignets

Makes 6 to 8 servings

Ingredients

Oil for frying
½ cup water
1 tablespoon active dry yeast
1 large egg
¼ cup granulated sugar
2 teaspoons vegetable oil
½ cup heavy cream
1 teaspoon pure banana extract

1 teaspoon vanilla extract
½ teaspoon butter vanilla extract
½ teaspoon citric acid
1 teaspoon baking powder
2 teaspoons kosher salt
2⅔ cups all purpose flour
4 ripe bananas, diced small
Vanilla ice cream

Banana Jam Ingredients

1 cup very ripe banana puree
⅔ cup granulated sugar
¼ teaspoon citric acid

1. Fill the fryer with oil and preheat to 350 degrees.

2. In a large bowl, combine water, yeast, egg and sugar; whisk using a hand whisk until the yeast is dissolved.

3. Whisk in the vegetable oil, cream, extracts, citric acid, baking powder and salt.

4. Using a spoon, stir in the flour and bananas; let rest for 20 minutes.

5. Using a small ice cream scoop, drop 6 scoops into the fryer.

6. Fry for 1 minute on each side or until puffed and golden brown.

7. Remove and drain on absorbent paper.

8. Repeat with remaining batter.

9. In a microwave-safe bowl, combine jam ingredients then microwave for 3 minutes or until it starts to boil.

10. Serve beignets topped with banana jam and a scoop of vanilla ice cream.

Canadian Beaver Tails

Makes 12 servings

Ingredients

¾ cup whole milk

6 large egg yolks

1 tablespoon vanilla extract

2¼ teaspoons active dry yeast

½ cup granulated sugar

1 teaspoon kosher salt

¼ cup powdered milk

2½ cups unbleached all purpose flour

½ cup cake flour, such as Swans Down

½ cup unsalted butter, softened

Canola oil for frying

Granulated sugar

1. Using a stand mixer on low speed combine the milk, yolks, vanilla, yeast, sugar, salt, powdered milk and both flours for 5 minutes.

2. Cover and let rest for 30 minutes.

3. Raise speed of the stand mixer to medium-low then slowly add the butter while mixing; continue to mix for 5 minutes.

4. Transfer the dough to an oiled extra-large plastic zipper bag then refrigerate for at least 4 hours.

5. Fill the fryer with oil and preheat to 350 degrees.

6. Remove the dough from the bag to a lightly floured surface then pat it into a 1/2-inch thick circle.

7. Using a cutter or a glass, cut the dough into 2-inch circles.

8. Stretch the circles into ovals then score each with a shallow cross-hatch design using a knife.

9. Let rest on the floured surface for 20 minutes.

10. Place an oval into the fryer; fry for 2 minutes, flip then fry for an additional minute or until golden brown.

11. Remove and drain on absorbent paper then roll in granulated sugar while still hot.

12. Repeat with remaining Beaver Tails and serve.

Amish Knee Patches

Makes 10 servings

Ingredients

Oil for frying, preferably canola oil
¾ cup heavy cream
1 large egg
2 teaspoons vanilla extract
¼ teaspoon butter vanilla extract
½ teaspoon kosher salt
2½ cups all purpose flour
Powdered or granulated sugar

These delightful, crispy confections get their quaint name from the way they are traditionally stretched; over a tea cloth-covered knee. The dough must be very thin and a knee is just the right shape to do the stretching. Another name for these is "Nothings" or "Elephant Ears." No matter which name they are called, the ingredients remain the same. They are traditionally made for Amish weddings during which platters of these pastries are stacked and placed on the same table as the wedding cake. Make sure that you don't overcook them. When fried correctly, they should be a very pale golden brown color.

1. Fill the fryer with oil and preheat to 375 degrees.

2. In a large bowl, combine the cream, egg, extracts, salt and flour; stir using a wooden spoon until a stiff, elastic dough ball forms.

3. Cut the dough into 10 pieces and roll each into a dough ball.

4. On a floured surface, roll out each ball using a rolling pin until very thin (about 1/16 inch).

5. Cut 3 small slits into the center of each piece.

6. Place one piece of dough into the fryer.

7. Fry for 1 minute on each side or until a very pale golden color is achieved.

8. Remove and drain on absorbent paper then dust with powdered sugar while still hot.

9. Repeat with remaining dough pieces and serve.

Churros

Makes 24 servings

Ingredients

1 cup water

1 cup evaporated milk

¼ teaspoon kosher salt

3 tablespoons granulated sugar

1 cup unsalted butter

1 teaspoon baking powder

2 teaspoons vanilla extract

2 cups bread flour

8 large eggs

Oil for frying

Cinnamon Sugar

Churros are sort of like the Spanish version of a straightened out French cruller. The dough used to make them is in the same family as crullers and is also similar to cream puff dough. Preparing them at home will make you wonder how you ever thought that the ones sold at state fairs or big club stores were any good. The difference is amazing. They are crispy, tender, light and sweet, with a hint of spiciness from the cinnamon.

1. In a large saucepan over medium-high heat, combine the water, evaporated milk, salt, sugar and butter; stir using a sturdy wooden spoon until a rolling boil is achieved.

2. While boiling, add the baking powder, vanilla and flour then stir vigorously until a dough ball forms.

3. Remove from heat and let cool for 5 minutes.

4. Using a hand mixer, beat the dough while adding the eggs one at a time; continue to beat until smooth.

5. Fill the fryer with oil and preheat to 350 degrees.

6. Transfer the mixture into a large pastry bag fitted with a large, open star tip.

7. Pipe churros onto rectangles of parchment paper until all the dough has been used up.

8. Place 2 churros on the parchment paper into the fryer; fry for 2 minutes on each side or until brown (remove parchment paper with tongs and discard).

9. Remove and drain on absorbent paper.

10. Roll warm churros in the cinnamon sugar.

11. Repeat with remaining churros and serve.

Custard Filled Long Johns

Makes 12 servings

Dough Ingredients

¾ cup whole milk

6 large egg yolks

1 tablespoon vanilla extract

2¼ teaspoons active dry yeast

½ cup granulated sugar

1 teaspoon kosher salt

¼ cup powdered milk

2½ cups unbleached all purpose flour

½ cup cake flour, such as Swans Down

½ cup unsalted butter, softened

Oil for frying, preferably canola

Powdered sugar

Microwave Custard Ingredients

6 egg yolks

½ cup granulated sugar

3 tablespoons cornstarch

1¾ cups whole milk

Seeds scraped from ½ vanilla bean

1. Using a stand mixer fitted with the dough hook, combine all dough ingredients, except butter, oil and powdered sugar; mix on low speed for 5 minutes.

2. Cover and let rest for 30 minutes.

3. Turn the speed to medium-low; slowly add the butter while mixing for an additional 5 minutes then transfer the dough to an oiled extra-large zipper bag and refrigerate for a minimum of 4 hours.

4. Fill the fryer with oil and preheat to 350 degrees.

5. Transfer the dough from the bag to a lightly floured surface then pat it into a 1/2-inch thick circle.

6. Using a sharp knife, cut the dough into 4x2-inch rectangles then let rest on the floured surface for 20 minutes.

7. Place 2 rectangles into the fryer; fry for 2 minutes on each side or until golden brown.

8. Remove and drain on absorbent paper then repeat with remaining rectangles.

9. To make the custard, combine the yolks, sugar and cornstarch in a microwave-safe bowl; whisk until smooth.

10. In a separate microwave-safe bowl, combine the milk and vanilla bean seeds.

11. Microwave the milk mixture for 3 minutes or until it boils.

12. Remove and pour it slowly into the yolk mixture while whisking fast until incorporated then microwave the combined mixture until it bubbles, stirring every minute.

13. Remove and let cool before using it to fill the Long Johns.

14. Top with powdered sugar and serve.

Crème Frite (Fried Cream)

Makes 6 to 8 servings

Ingredients

1½ cups heavy cream

2½ cups whole milk, divided

Seeds scraped from 1 vanilla bean

2 tablespoons unsalted butter

½ cup cornstarch

2 tablespoons all purpose flour

½ cup sugar

½ teaspoon kosher salt

6 large egg yolks

Oil for frying

1 cup all purpose flour

2 large eggs, beaten

1½ cups vanilla wafers, finely ground

2 cups raspberries

½ cup powdered sugar

1. In a large saucepan over medium heat, combine the heavy cream, 1½ cups milk, vanilla beans, and butter; bring to a simmer.

2. In a large bowl, combine 1 cup milk, cornstarch, flour, sugar, salt and yolks.

3. Slowly pour the hot cream mixture into the cornstarch mixture while whisking fast.

4. Pour the combined mixture back into the saucepan; cook until it reaches 165 degrees on a thermometer then pour the mixture into a 9x13 inch pan, cover and refrigerate for 2 hours.

5. Fill the fryer with oil and preheat to 375 degrees.

6. Place the flour into a shallow bowl, pour the eggs into a separate bowl and spread the wafer crumbs in a third bowl.

7. Cut the chilled cream mixture into small diamond-shaped pieces.

8. Coat the pieces with flour, dip them in egg then roll them in crumbs until coated.

9. Place a few pieces into the fryer; fry for 1 minute or until light golden brown.

10. Remove and drain on absorbent paper then repeat with remaining pieces.

11. In a pitcher, combine the raspberries and powdered sugar; blend using an immersion blender until smooth then serve with the Crème Frite.

Funnel Cakes with Tart Cherry Topping

Makes 4 servings

Cherry Topping Ingredients

1½ cups frozen tart red cherries, thawed
⅓ cup granulated sugar
1 tablespoon cornstarch

Funnel Cake Ingredients

Oil for frying
2 cups cake flour
1 cup all purpose flour
2 teaspoons baking powder
½ teaspoon kosher salt
2 tablespoons granulated sugar
2 large eggs, beaten
4 tablespoons vegetable oil
2 cups club soda, cold
Powdered sugar

1. In a microwave-safe bowl, combine the topping ingredients; stir well.

2. Microwave for 6 minutes or until bubbly then remove from the microwave.

3. Fill the fryer with oil and preheat to 375 degrees.

4. In a bowl, combine remaining funnel cake ingredients, except powdered sugar.

5. Whisk until fairly smooth and only a few lumps remain then pour the batter into a squeeze bottle or small pitcher.

6. Lower the fryer basket into the oil.

7. Squirt long lines of batter into the oil, swirling them over each other in a zig-zag pattern to connect the batter to itself; use about ½ cup of batter for each funnel cake.

8. Use a small spatula to carefully loosen the batter from the wires of the fryer basket then turn over the funnel cake using tongs and fry until golden brown.

9. Remove and drain on absorbent paper then repeat with remaining batter.

10. Serve the funnel cakes topped with cherry topping and powdered sugar.

Gooey Chocolate Purses

Makes 6 servings

Ganache Ingredients

1 cup heavy cream
1½ cups semi-sweet chocolate chips

Ingredients

Oil for frying, preferably canola
6 spring roll wrappers
1 cup pecan pieces, toasted
1 cup fresh raspberries
6 strips (8 inches each) kitchen twine
Powdered sugar

1. In a microwave-safe bowl, microwave the cream until bubbly.

2. Place the chocolate chips into a bowl then pour the hot cream over the chocolate; let rest for 5 minutes.

3. Stir chocolate until completely dissolved and mixture is shiny; refrigerate to cool.

4. Pour oil into the fryer and preheat to 375 degrees.

5. Place a spring roll wrapper flat on the counter.

6. Remove the ganache from the refrigerator and place a tablespoon-sized ball of ganache in the center of the wrapper; top with pecan pieces and raspberries.

7. Lift the sides of the wrapper, shape it into a purse then pinch and tie the bundle with a piece of kitchen twine.

8. Repeat with remaining ingredients then chill in the freezer for 10 minutes.

9. Place 2 purses into the fryer; fry for 1 minute or until light golden brown.

10. Remove and drain on absorbent paper then repeat with remaining purses.

11. Use kitchen shears to snip and remove the twine.

12. Top with powdered sugar and garnish with any remaining raspberries or pecans.

13. Microwave remaining ganache for a few seconds and serve with the purses.

Homemade Cannoli

Makes 12 cannoli

Dough Ingredients

2½ cups all purpose flour
¼ cup granulated sugar
1 teaspoon kosher salt
1 teaspoon ground cinnamon
½ cup unsalted butter, softened
1 large egg, beaten
⅓ cup Marsala wine
1 tablespoon apple cider vinegar
Oil for frying
12 wooden dowels (see tools page 8)

Filling Ingredients

16 ounces fresh ricotta cheese
⅓ cup granulated sugar
½ teaspoon vanilla extract
2 drops almond extract
½ cup semi-sweet chocolate chips
½ cup slivered pistachio nuts, toasted
Powdered sugar

1. In a large bowl, combine all dough ingredients, except oil for frying and wooden dowels; mix using a wooden spoon until a smooth dough forms then wrap and chill the dough for 30 minutes.

2. Fill the fryer with oil and preheat to 350 degrees; if your dowels are new, fry them for 5 minutes to season them first.

3. Roll out the dough until 1/16-inch thick then cut out 12 circles, 3 inches each.

4. Wrap a circle of dough around a cooled dowel, pinching the ends to seal; repeat with remaining dough circles.

5. Place a few cannoli shells on the dowels into the fryer; fry for 4 minutes or until dark brown.

6. Remove and drain on absorbent paper; let cool, twist out the dowels then repeat with remaining shells.

7. Purée the ricotta cheese in a food processor for 1 minute or until smooth then add the sugar and extracts to the food processor; process to incorporate.

8. Transfer the mixture to a pastry bag fitted with a 1/2-inch open tip.

9. Pipe mixture into the shells then dip the ends in chocolate chips and pistachio nuts.

10. Top with powdered sugar and serve.

Malassadas

Makes 14 servings

Ingredients

3 cups all purpose flour
¼ cup granulated sugar
1 tablespoon + ½ teaspoon active dry yeast
6 large eggs, divided
¼ cup evaporated milk
1 tablespoon kosher salt

12 ounces unsalted butter, softened
1 teaspoon vanilla extract
1 teaspoon apple cider vinegar
Oil for frying
Granulated or powdered sugar

1. In a stand mixer fitted with the dough hook, combine the flour, sugar, and yeast; mix on medium speed.

2. While mixing, add two eggs and the evaporated milk until a paste forms then add remaining eggs (one at a time).

3. Continue to mix the dough for 5 minutes; add the salt, butter, vanilla and vinegar then mix for an additional 2 minutes.

4. Remove the bowl from the stand mixer; remove the hook, cover with plastic wrap and refrigerate the dough for 2 hours.

5. Place the dough onto a floured surface.

6. Divide the dough into 14 pieces then form each piece into a ball.

7. Cover the balls with a soft towel and let rise for 25 minutes.

8. Fill the fryer with oil and preheat to 375 degrees.

9. Place a few balls into the fryer; fry for 1 minute on each side or until golden brown.

10. Remove and drain on absorbent paper then repeat with remaining dough.

11. Roll them in sugar and serve warm.

Crullers

Makes 24 servings

Ingredients

Oil for frying
2 cups whole milk
1 teaspoon kosher salt
1 tablespoon granulated sugar
1 cup unsalted butter

½ teaspoon baking powder
1 teaspoon vanilla extract
2 cups all purpose flour
8 large eggs

Glaze Ingredients

2½ cups powdered sugar
¾ cup heavy cream
2 teaspoons vanilla extract

1. Fill the fryer with oil and preheat to 375 degrees.

2. In a large saucepan over medium heat, combine the milk, salt, sugar and butter; bring to a rolling boil.

3. Add the baking powder, vanilla and all purpose flour all at once; stir using a wooden spoon until a smooth dough ball forms around the spoon then remove from heat and let cool for 5 minutes.

4. Using a hand mixer, add the eggs (one at a time) and beat to incorporate.

5. In a bowl, combine the glaze ingredients; whisk until smooth then set it aside.

6. Cut 24 squares (3 inches each) of parchment paper.

7. Transfer the dough to a pastry bag fitted with a large open star tip; pipe the dough into circles onto the parchment squares, overlapping the ends to secure.

8. Place 3 crullers on their parchment squares into the fryer; using tongs, remove the parchment from the crullers and discard then fry for 2 minutes on each side or until browned.

9. Remove and drain on absorbent paper then repeat with remaining crullers.

10. Dip crullers into the glaze and let excess glaze drip into the bowl before serving.

Old Fashioned Yeast Raised Doughnuts

Makes 12 servings

Ingredients

½ cup whole milk

⅓ cup unsalted butter

⅓ cup granulated sugar

1½ teaspoons kosher salt

2 cups all purpose flour, divided

2 packages active dry yeast

⅓ cup water

2 large eggs

1½ cups cake flour

2 cups powdered sugar, sifted

⅓ cup heavy cream

Pinch of kosher salt

½ teaspoon vanilla extract

Oil for frying

1. In a saucepan over medium heat, combine milk, butter, sugar and salt; bring to a simmer.

2. Pour the mixture into a large bowl, let cool until slightly warm then add 1 cup of all purpose flour and beat well using a mixer.

3. Add the yeast, water, and eggs to the bowl; mix until combined then add remaining flours and mix to form a soft dough that pulls away from the sides of the bowl.

4. Place the dough into a large oiled mixing bowl; roll the dough in the bowl until oiled on all sides then cover and refrigerate for a minimum of 3 hours.

5. On a lightly floured surface, roll out the dough until 1/3-inch thick then cut it using a floured doughnut cutter; transfer to a lightly floured baking pan and let rest for 40 minutes or until it rises to double its size.

6. In a bowl, combine remaining ingredients, except oil; set aside the glaze.

7. Fill the fryer with oil and preheat to 375 degrees.

8. Place 3 doughnuts into the fryer; fry for 1 minute on each side or until golden brown.

9. Remove and drain on a cooling rack with absorbent paper underneath then repeat with remaining doughnuts.

10. Dip the doughnuts in the glaze while still warm then return them to the cooling rack until ready to serve.

Pink Feather Boas

Makes 15 servings

Doughnut Ingredients

1 package active dry yeast
1½ cups whole milk
2 teaspoons kosher salt
3 tablespoons granulated sugar
2 tablespoons unsalted butter, softened
4 cups all purpose flour
Oil for frying

Glaze Ingredients

2 cups powdered sugar
A tiny pinch of kosher salt
⅓ cup heavy cream
¼ teaspoon vanilla extract
2 drops red food coloring

Coconut Ingredients

1 cup sweetened coconut flakes
A few drops red food coloring

1. Using a stand mixer fitted with the dough hook, combine doughnut ingredients, except oil; mix on low speed for 7 minutes or until a smooth dough forms.

2. Transfer the dough to a lightly floured surface then knead until a rough ball is formed; transfer the dough to a clean, greased bowl then cover and let rest for 1½ hours or until it rises to double its size.

3. Place the dough onto a lightly floured surface then roll it out until ½-inch thick.

4. Cut the dough using a doughnut cutter then place the doughnuts as well as holes onto a floured cookie sheet; cover with a soft towel and let rise for 30 minutes.

5. Fill the fryer with oil and preheat to 360 degrees.

6. Place 2 doughnuts and 2 holes into the fryer; fry for 2 minutes on each side or until golden brown.

7. Remove and drain on a cooling rack with absorbent paper underneath then repeat with remaining doughnuts.

8. In a bowl, combine the glaze ingredients; stir well.

9. Combine the coconut ingredients in a large zipper bag; shake until the color is evenly distributed.

10. Dip the doughnuts first in glaze then in colored coconut before serving.

Spudnuts (Cake Doughnuts)

Makes 15 doughnuts

Ingredients

3½ cups all purpose flour

1 teaspoon kosher salt

4 teaspoons baking powder

½ teaspoon ground cinnamon

¼ teaspoon freshly grated nutmeg

3 tablespoons unsalted butter, melted

2 teaspoons vanilla extract

2 large eggs

¾ cup granulated sugar

1½ cups cooked Russet potatoes, mashed

½ cup whole milk

Oil for frying

Favorite toppings

Spudnut is the affectionate name given to these doughnuts that are cake doughnuts, not yeast or raised doughnuts. The addition of potato is wonderful, just like in so many yeast breads and baked goods. Potatoes add lightness, a silky texture and an indescribable mellow taste.

1. In a large bowl, combine the flour, salt, baking powder, cinnamon and nutmeg.

2. In a second bowl, combine the butter, vanilla, eggs, sugar, potatoes and milk; whisk until smooth, pour the potato mixture into the flour mixture, stir until a dough forms then cover and chill for at least 1 hour.

3. Fill the fryer with oil and preheat to 375 degrees.

4. On a floured counter, roll the dough until 1/2-inch thick then cut it into rings using a doughnut cutter or drinking glass.

5. Place 2 Spudnuts and 2 holes into the fryer; fry for 2 minutes or until golden brown, remove and drain on absorbent paper then repeat with remaining ingredients.

6. Top doughnuts with the chocolate ganache on page 138 or the glaze on page 148 then decorate with toppings as desired and serve.

Vanilla Rosettes

Makes 25 rosettes

Ingredients

Oil for frying
1 cup whole milk
1 large egg
Pinch of kosher salt
2 tablespoons granulated sugar

1 teaspoon vanilla extract
Pinch of butter vanilla extract
1 cup all purpose flour
Powdered sugar

When I was growing up in the Congo, my Mom would sometimes make these scrumptiously delicate cookies for us. She would stand at the old wood burning stove for what seemed to be hours. Mom's rosette iron was an old cast-iron affair with a red handle. It came with all sorts of patterns and shapes for making cookies. She would let us select our favorite shape to dip into the thin batter then carefully lower it into the bubbling oil to form the cookies. I always chose the daisy shape and it is still my favorite.

1. Fill the fryer with oil and preheat to 365 degrees.

2. In a bowl, combine remaining ingredients, except powdered sugar; pour mixture through a fine strainer until smooth.

3. Assemble the rosette iron (see tools page 8) with your favorite design then heat the rosette iron in the fryer for 1 minute; remove and blot lightly using absorbent paper.

4. Carefully dip the rosette iron into the batter so that it comes 3/4 of the way up the mold (it is important not to cover the mold entirely with batter or it will not come off easily).

5. Place the rosette iron into the fryer; fry for 1 minute or until the rosette floats freely and the bottom is brown.

6. Use tongs or a chopstick to turn the rosette over to brown the other side; fry until browned on both sides then remove and drain on absorbent paper.

7. Top with powdered sugar while still hot then repeat with remaining batter and serve.

For more of Marian's tips and ideas, please visit:
www.mariangetz.com